Achieving Millennium Development Goals Through Edeh's Activities and Philosophy

Associate Professor Eneh

authorHOUSE®

AuthorHouse™
1663 Liberty Drive
Bloomington, IN 47403
www.authorhouse.com
Phone: 1 (800) 839-8640

Published by AuthorHouse 06/03/2015

ISBN: 978-1-5049-1335-5 (sc)
ISBN: 978-1-5049-1334-8 (e)

Contents

Chapter Three

List of Contributors

1. Sr. Purissima Egbekpalu SJS Ph.D- Lecturer Madonna University, Nigeria

2. Rev Joseph Mbave (FJS) - Benue State

3. Associate Professor Eneh- Lecturer Madonna University, Nigeria

4. Charles C. Onuh - Enugu State

5. Rev Isaac Nginga (FJS) - Benue State

6. Rev Oliver O. Ugwu (FJS) - Enugu State

General Introduction

It is a statement of fact to assert that the human existence is shrouded in complex elements. Man, from the cradle of his life, is continuously cut up in a web of situations that leave him in the cross-road of deciding whether to continue living or to quit his bewildering experiences. The truth value of this position lies in a proper consideration of human history; it bears a heavy burden of awful events and indices ranging from micro-situations such as high level of poverty, illiteracy, preventable break-outs of epidemics that leave many dead, socio-political unrest to a high level of mortality rate. Further, apart from these social malaises that continuously punctuate world events and question the rationality of man, there also exist natural disasters amongst which are; tsunami, earthquake, fire out-break, erosions, and other natural mishaps that plunge many into unimaginable abyss of excruciating pains and difficulties. Those ugly phenomena culminate into making the world unfavourable for many; while many have taken suicide as an option, others live at the brink of unhappiness and misfortune.

Sequel to the above claim, the onus of transforming the world into a comfort zone and an inhabitable environment has, for all ages, been the sole responsibility of humans. Hence, the explosive inventions in areas of science, technology, arts, religion, and other spheres of human endeavour explain man's struggle to create a better world and live happily in it. Even the various cooperative bodies and international organisations are all geared towards the same mission.

Consequent upon that, the United Nations in the year 2000 came up with eight strategic goals drawn from key areas of human existence including extreme poverty, education, health, global partnership, and their aligns. These goals have been billed to be actualized in or before 2015.

Furthermore, following the United Nation's declaration of the eight Millennium Development Goals (MDG), various governments, non-governmental organisations, cooperate organisations, institutions, and private individuals have woken up from their existential slumber to tackle squarely these ugly realities that have continued to menace the human family. It is in this same spirit that authorities of Madonna University decided to dedicate this year's International Convention of Intellectuals and Experts to the actualization of the Millennium Development Goals with a special reference to the contributions of the Founder, Very Rev Fr Prof Emmanuel Matthew Paul Edeh C.S.Sp OFR. This book, therefore is a brainchild of the said convention. This book is divided into four chapters.

Chapter one, entitled *Edeh's Social Philosophy: An Indispensable Trail to Peace and Sustainable Development,* is a composite of papers presented by Rev Sr Dr Purissima Egbekpalu and Brother Joseph Mbave. In this paper, the duo establish that Edeh's philosophy constitutes the bedrock foundation upon which his irreplaceable contributions to the betterment of the human conditions are built. In this philosophy, there is a proper understanding of the true ontological nature of man as "good that is," or *mmadi*, which explains why he should be loved and cared for. This care, according to the presenters, finds its full realization in a community of love which is itself held together by *ome nani* (tradition). They conclude by positing Edeh as having brought peace to the lives of many through the interplay of thought and action that characterizes his social philosophy (*EPTAism*).

Chapter two comprises the papers presented by Associate Professor Eneh and Onu Charles. The chapter entitled *Edeh's Proactive Approach*

Towards the Actualization of the MDGs centers on Edeh's practical contributions to the amelioration of human suffering, especially through education empowerment and eradication of extreme poverty and hunger.

In chapter three, attempt is made to expose Edeh's further activities geared towards the same mission of wiping the tears of suffering off the face of many but special emphasis on sustainable healthcare. This chapter constitutes the papers presented by Isaac Nginga and Oliver Onyeka Ugwu.

Chapter four is dedicated to the general conclusion.

Chapter One

EDEH'S SOCIAL PHILOSOPHY: AN INDISPENSABLE TRAIL TO PEACE AND SUSTAINABLE DEVELOPMENT

By
Sr. Purissima Egbepkalu SJS Ph.D and Joseph Mbave

INTRODUCTION

Positive and progressive development is the dream of every individual community and the nation at large. But this cannot be achieved in the midst of wars and misunderstanding. The same history vividly showed that development is impeded through violence. Peace is a major catalyst that avails and sustains proper development. And so the question remains: how can genuine peace be attained? In his philosophy of man, Edeh made us to understand that peace is possible through man's understanding of himself as peaceful experience starts with every single individual and extends to others as encapsulated in his philosophy of *mmadi*.

In this philosophy, the origin of humans (good that is) is the supreme "good in se" (God), and thus man derives his goodness by participating in the goodness of God. The combination of all these factors forms Edeh's social philosophy. Since the ontological nature of man, according to Edeh, positions man as an extension of his Maker "good in se",

Edeh's social philosophy, by extension, prescribes the imperative of treating *mmadi* with dignity and love, thus consolidating peace and development in the human society.

Before exposing and discussing the specific ways that Edeh's social philosophy would impact on the society, we will take a look at three important concepts of Edeh's social philosophy: Community, Omenani (tradition), *EPTAism*/ECPM.

Community in Edeh

Every human being lives in a society and human society is made up of communities. When Aristotle, the ancient Greek philosopher and one of the greatest thinkers of all time, says that man is a social animal, he is referring to the need for man to live in society and the inability of individual humans to be completely self-sufficient. Aristotle sees society as good and worthy place for the development and welfare of humans. Logically, Edeh's notion of community is influenced by the Igbo thought and pattern. His experience of the Igbo milieu shaped his sense of community is seen and informed the philosophy set down in *Towards an Igbo Metaphysics*. In this traditional Igbo milieu, a community engenders the spirit of unity engage and brotherhood— evidence of interdependence between *mmadi* and the community. He says: "In an Igbo community which embodies traditional culture, there is cooperation among people residing permanently in a single locality. The members of such a community share the basic conditions of common life" (Edeh, 1985, 56–57). This is the type of community where *mmadi* fares well, as people in society cooperate. For Edeh, we ought to live in and cooperate with the community while we still maintain our personal identity. He notes that "the community strives to maintain the different groups within it while maintaining itself as a community. Hence, the life and purpose of the community come, in certain matters, before the individual interests of the members" (1985, 57). Thus, the community Edeh advocates is a community of interdependent human beings who accommodate one another to serve the greater good.

Aristotle's view of man as a social animal seems to agree with Edeh on this point, as Aristotle sees man's growth and survival as dependant on his relationship with the society. *Mmadi* contributes naturally to the community while the community aids *mmadi* and maintains the good in good that is. Edeh (1985) corroborates this point by stressing that in the Igbo traditional context, life, and existence belong equally to the community of being formed by dead ancestors and to the people who are still alive. Above all, life belongs to Chineke, the maker, author, provider, and sustainer of life and existence in its entirety. To stress the logic of Edeh's philosophical anthropology in its application to the achievement of world peace, Egbekpalu (2011) reasons that God, good in se, created all human beings to partake in His goodness, that every person, irrespective of colour, race, education, religion, or other differences partakes in the same ultimate destiny. Furthermore, since all people originate from God, everyone created by the same God should live harmoniously in the same world as a result of our shared origin. In today's world, we have become highly constrained by artificial constructs including racism, ethnocentrism, nepotism, and hatred, and these barriers are opposed to the healthy development of any society. Rather than work with a harmonious, brotherly, communal spirit in the philosophy of Edeh, some people, out of ignorance, have lost touch with their ontological realities, thereby jeopardizing the nexus with their final destination. Many other selfish people of the Contemporary Age are trying to transmute themselves into lifeless, mechanical entities and demigods in disharmony with the human status of good that is. To overcome this negativity, we must nurture community as Edeh sees it, we must nurture it with the flavour of communalism and inspiration of Chineke, the origin of *mmadi* and author of the universe and as a quest for an unbreakable existential unity of life, a communion of *mmadi* with society and the maker of the universe. Edeh's concept of community abhors individualism, since individualism truncates the unity and comprehensiveness of human life and truncates the true nature of humans. In Edeh's notion of communal existence, we see ourselves and the world at large as two inseparable sides of the same coin. In addition, we are dependent on society and morally obliged to help society. In this communal cohabitation, everyone is expected to uphold the integrity of the other to ensure the symmetrical welfare of all. As Egonu (2005) remarks, humanity must remind itself, in view of modern science and technology, of the sacredness of human life, the joy of living, the beauty of creation, and the responsibility of all to protect all to cooperate to promote the common good.

Omenani in Edeh

Having seen Edeh's concept of community, it is now vital that we should bring the concept of *omenani*, or tradition, into the discourse. Africans in general live a group life, as reflected in extended family system, existence of various traditional social institutions, including age grades, women's groups, councils of elders, councils of titled men, and villages or town unions. The peculiarity of these groups lies in the strong ties that bind their members in and the relationship their members have with one another and the larger another society, coupled with the sacrifice members make for the sustenance of their groups and their effective use of these units as agents of socialization.

The Aristotelian affirmation that man is a social animal is once again social evident in African worldview, bringing into light the efforts made by average African to preserve the community by establishing strong bonds with the nuclear family, extended family, social groups and the community in general, as these ties consolidate solidarity among members of the society. Africans are strongly attached to family and they believe that home is always the best, and the number of years they live in a foreign land in no way negates their ties to this origin.

For the Igbos of West Africa, the ties to home are so strong that when an Igbo man dies in a foreign land, his corpse must be sent back to his hometown and his father's compound where he would be given a proper burial so that he may continue his journey with his ancestors. Even if an Igbo man lives oversees, he still makes financial and other material contributions to the sustenance of his home community. His separation by distance does not undermine his share of strong emotions for, obligations to, and attachment to his people.

Tradition is the entirety of relationships of a people and their cultural traits, attitudes, tendencies, and lifestyle transferred from one generation to another. No community exists without tradition and it provides the standards, norms, and values that define the people's ways of life. The Igbo community is patterned by Igbo tradition.

Thanks to tradition, people are bound not only by biology but also by social relationships, interdependence, and mutual expectations. Edeh understands the importance of tradition in the Igbo worldview, noting that "community is structured the way it is on account of Igbo adherence to the stipulations of tradition" (Edeh 1985, 58), and this has also influenced his social philosophy. He knows that tradition is needed for a cohesive and peaceful society. *Omenani* is the Igbo term for "tradition," and it is a strong binding force for the Igbos. The fundamental question here is: what is the relationship between *omenani* and community? They are inseparable, since no community can exist without customs and tradition, but customs and tradition cannot exist without a particular human community.

In fact, to live in the Igbo community without the concept of *omenani* would be like living in a house without a strong foundation. In Igbo language, *ani* means land, ground, or soil and Edeh reminds us that the word is also used for the Earth goddess, which the Igbos regard as the highest and most universal goddess in Igboland. In this direction, the Earth (*ani/ala*) is a symbol of beauty and moral good according to Edeh and as a result, it is revered as a goddess in Igboland as it is in many other cultures. Thus, Edeh defines *omenani* as "an inherited pattern of thought and action customarily and mysteriously in harmony with the dynamic creativity of being with the totality of all that is" (1985, 59).

An important point here is that *omenani* connotes action—practices in consonance with the virtues and values of the land and the will of the Earth goddess, the "terrestrial expression of Chineke, the all-embracing supra-sensory being" (Edeh 1985, 59). Thus, *omenani* is synonymous with order, concordance, justice, unity, and peace. *Omenani* is emblematic of the Igbos' shared ideals of what is just and right. It is a reminder to humanity that irrespective of ethnicity, colour, or geographical location, humans are ontologically the same; each person is like other people because of our ontological oneness even though we still maintain our individuality which renders every person unlike any other one.

The truth of the matter is that *omenani* gives meaning to Igbo life, which guarantees the people's survival and corporate unity. Edeh (1985) also explains that the spirit of *omenani* is always in accord with the sense of mystery and the supernatural with the idea of keeping all in tune with the community of being. *Omenani* therefore is in association with the sensory and visible as well as the suprasensory and invisible, all in relationship with the thoughts and actions of the people. This concept of the harmony of existence is consistently vivid, whether the people are thinking and acting as a community or as individuals. If Plato could describe the state as a family as seen in the Republic, how much more the Igbos, whose social co-habitation is inspired by the spirit of *omenani*? *Omenani* gives the Igbos a sense of family, community, coherence, and identity.

Evil is in opposition to *omenani*: "Whether an evil is an offence against anyone or anything, whether it is an occurrence among the living, the dead, or gods, the Igbos see it as a removal of an aspect of the well-being and completeness of *omenani*" (Edeh, 1985, 104). Since *omenani* is an inherited pattern of thought and action that is mysteriously in harmony with the totality of all that is, Edeh furthermore elucidates: "As a clarification of this, we must add that *omenani* is a generic term for the body of Igbo socio-religious laws, customs and traditions, passed from generation to generation and handed down to the ancestors from God,

Chukwu, through the Earth-god. For the Igbos, an evil is regarded as an offence against *omenani*" (Edeh, 1985, 103).

Omenani is actually the source of the people's cohesion and value; it is equally the pillar of their common good. Edeh says, "Man must form a union in order to enter into communion with other men in order to safeguard his own existence. This was the intention of the founders of Igbo society" (Edeh, 1985, 106). Since man lives in the community, his actions are not done in isolation. He forms part of the wholeness of life and *omenani* does not allow him to break this existential unity that binds the living and the dead with the Supreme Being, Chineke, who cares for all and maintains divine order.

Edeh's Philosophy of Thought and Action (*EPTAism*) and Edeh's Charity Peace Model (ECPM)

Because of this derivation of our nature from the absolute good, it becomes necessary that we treat one another well in both theoretical and practical terms. When this is done, peace will prevail and the good nature of humans will reign. It is this desire for permanent peace that led Edeh to develop his Philosophy of Thought and Action (*EPTAism*). It is to be underscored that the originality of Edeh's philosophy is its ability to synchronize thought and action through which he broke the jinx of philosophical method. This concrete and practical actualization of theoretical science that is a significant feature of African philosophy is what he called *EPTAism*. In his words, "After the presentation of the African metaphysical thought pattern, one must go further to show a concrete and practical actualization of this. In the same manner, arriving at the God-man-world scheme that characterizes African philosophy leads one to the practical actualization in interplay between thought and action. This is what can be called *EPTAism*, that is, Edeh's Philosophy of Thought and Action.

Since *EPTAism* is peace oriented, Edeh accordingly devised a model of peace to complement it: Edeh's Charity Peace Model (ECPM). A fusion of *EPTAism* and ECPM Peace makes Edeh's mission of practical and effective charity concrete. We can understand the ECPM in this way: "It is a model of peace that is anchored in practical and effective charity. The practical and effective charity is further rooted in the philosophy of man (*mmadi*) "good that is" philosophy espoused by Edeh.

Edeh's presentation of African metaphysical thought is not enough in his view, that is why he goes on to demonstrate a concrete and practical realization of that philosophy, thereby arriving at an interaction of thought and action. "Thus this is what can be called *EPTAism,* that is, Edeh's Philosophy of Thought and Action" (Edeh, 2009), *EPTAism* also leads us to an African concept of theology that God exists and humans lean on him for survival, something that Africans experience in daily life and form religious practices around. Edeh (2009) explains that the need to present African philosophy as an ideal of human existence and human dignity, along with his life experience and his belief that all beings created by God are ontologically good, spurred his mission of practical and effective charity. To bring peace to the world, we must approach people without segregation or prejudice and Edeh's sense of charity embraces the downtrodden, the sick, the poor, the abandoned and the victims of social maladies. In short, Edeh's charity alleviates humans' ugly situations. In the Igbo thought pattern, God, Chineke, not only creates but continues to be present in the creature. He is Chi-ukwu, the Big God and the Greatest Chi (God), for no greater chi could be thought of. God is also Osebuluwa, who cares, loves, supports and consistently caters to the needs of humans and aids us in the actualization of the ultimate end of our existence. Thus: "If God as Osebuluwa cares and supports man to the realization of his purpose, I must care and support my fellow man to the realization of his purpose, and this leads to peace in his heart, peace in the society and to the modern world" (Edeh, 2009, 49). Edeh therefore believes that the next step is to concretize this endeavour through practical and effective charity. Unfortunately, we have reached an age of civilization in which we have mistaken ourselves for God. Our accomplishments in science and advancements in technology have regrettably given us a sense that we have arrived by efforts devoid of any supratemporal intervention. This know-it-all ego has invariably created a gulf between us and our maker. The same loss of our sense of origin has contributed to the modern idea that man is a means, an object and an element, rather than an end, a subject, and a person. Wars, ethnic clashes, international conflicts, homicide, genocide and other forms of violence easily trace their sources in humanity's withdrawal from our Creator. If we lose our connection with Chineke, the "good in se," we also lose our own goodness, becoming void of our own nature, as a result we finally become *mmadi*-less. When *mmadi* is removed from Chineke, he automatically lacks the completeness of his being and in this case, acting in accord with his original state as good that is becomes impossible.

ECPM is a reinstatement of the authentic relationship between human and human and between human and God. In order to realize the essence of creation, we must be connected to the supreme good and our own *mmadi*. It is not sufficient to explain this verbally because this reality must be practiced and lived. Edeh's Charity Peace Model is the practicalization of our goodness in our relationships with others in other to achieve a genuine peace. The goodness of God is best acknowledged when man is treated as that which he is by nature, good that is. It is impossible for anyone to genuinely love God and venerate Him without extending care and love to others.

A critical look at the concept of charity in the ECPM, gives it credit for being a model concerned with how one hearkens to reason as a conscientious moral agent by seeking the good of everyone. The deontological nature of human good and morality is important because it mandates us to do good, perform practical charity because there is an intrinsic good in doing so. Charity, according to Edeh, also goes beyond almsgiving, which is only of secondary importance.

Edeh's form of charity is imbued with African philosophy, a lived philosophy, a philosophy of human experience with no room for duality between thought and action. This inseparableness of thought and action in Edeh's philosophy is evident in Edeh's Philosophy of Thought and Action (*EPTAism*), which has also developed into a school of thought. The moment we realize that God is the ultimate cause of our existence; we will have no option than to act in harmony with *mmadi*, as designed by God.

Edeh insists that man should wake up from his slumber and understand first that God is the ultimate cause of his existence, that his nature as *mmadi* is divinely ordained by God in unity with his ultimate reality and the purpose of his existence. Man cannot run away from this fact because he cannot pretend that his being is purposeless. He cannot equate himself with lower creatures and abandon his exalted position as the king of the temporal realm in a permanent rapport with the Ultimate Good (God).

Edeh's Philosophy: A Concrete Existential Treatise

The ingenuity of Edeh's philosophy is not just the first articulation of African philosophy but most importantly, the worth of such enunciation; its practicability in man's concrete existence. Hence, it is a lived philosophy drawn from the experiences of the cultural values of African people but which can be extended to other peoples and races as it addresses the existential hub of the generality of human beings; a meaningful life of healthy and lovely intrapersonal, interpersonal, communal, and international relationships. As such, it exhumes how theoretical science is inextricably intermingled with practical experiential existence of man. In this way, it proffers an ideal way of dealing with man's life departing from African experience with regard to respecting human dignity.

His "Peace to the Modern World" which he dedicated to all seekers of peace addresses the existential realities and points to a way forward in the concrete living of the prescriptions of the African philosophy of being, summarily as responding to the practical existential rhythms of life according to man's nature.

Edeh's Peace Concept as an Irreversible Path towards Long-Term Development: Can development be sustained at all in this world of constant conflicts, terrorism, etc? Edeh's peace concept has the answer and it is very optimistic about it.

The logic of Edeh's philosophy of PEACEFUL convivum as a CATALYST to SUSTAINABLE DEVELOPMENT can be thus depicted:

God

Love, Care and Respect

Man   Man

Peaceful convivum

Human development

(Collective Consciousness)

National Development

(not by force but by understanding)

Inter-national Development

The above illustration simply implies that with Edeh's philosophy, God is the foundation of man's being. As the ultimate source of life, he cares, nurtures, and provides for man. Man's goal in life and principles of his existence are therefore derived from this fact of creation and the relationship between the creator and the created and even by implication among the created themselves. This is to say that man's activities must correspond to his *raison d'etre*. And what is this *raison d'etre*? Edeh's philosophy reveals that it is to share in the nature of the Being that posits him. What then is the nature of that Being? It consists among other attributes in caring, loving and providing for the created for he is GOOD. Man therefore is by nature invited to appropriate this action of loving and caring in his daily existence because he partakes in the goodness of his creator.

Unless man understands his goal of his existence within this context of love and care and practices them as our philosopher urges him, he may be acting against his nature (*contra natura*) and creating disorder both in himself and in the society in which he lives. This disorder can be interpreted as conflict, war, etc. To this effect, conflict, war, hatred, and the like are not in keeping with the value of human nature. So understood, love for God, oneself and for another is then the only way to actualize oneself, attain one's purpose of existence, and consequently bring order into one's life as well as the entire society.

In this sense, the order experienced becomes peace and peace is the only rudiment that consolidates the foundation of development, leads to its progressive success, and assures its sustenance. In keeping with the principles of loving harmony of thought and action, people can then commit to better and more meaningful lives that paves way to transparent democratic culture with collaborative initiatives that builds the nation positively, pursues concrete projects that consolidate peace while keeping the economy on a sound footing for the achievement of the millennium developmental goals and promotion of human dignity.

Until we realize these and grasp others in the innermost core of our personalities, the spirit of selfishness and disintegration will always pave way to incessant abuse of power, social crumbling, pervasive poverty, food insecurity, poor leadership, debilitated justice structure, limited job opportunities, abductions, and all sorts of degenerative factors that thwarts development and demotes human dignity.

Conclusion

Edeh's philosophy of thought and action as analysed above proves that positive acknowledgment of God and neighbors through love gives existential meaning to man's life, actualizes the true nature of and purpose of his existence. This definitely leads to genuine peace which on its side is a catalyst to sustainable development at all spheres of life. This philosophical position therefore invites us all to deeper understanding of our common goal in life; to live and love one another as creatures with common creator, same purpose and collective existential goal. Therefore, we consciously harmonize our good thoughts with good actions when we realized that the peace which Edeh made us to understand cannot be attained by force but can be achieved through reciprocal love This then becomes a reality and accomplishment of the millennium for the sustenance of our collective achievements.

Bibliography

Edeh, E.M.P, The Pilgrimage Centre of Eucharistic Adoration. Uk, Minuteman Press, 1997.

Edeh, E.M.P, Igbo Metaphysics: The First Articulation of African Philosophy of Being, Madonna University Publications, Enugu, Nigeria, 2009.

Edeh, E.M.P., Peace to the Modern World: A Way forward Through the Concrete Living of the Existential Dictates of the African Philosophy of Being, UK, Minuteman Press, 2007.

Edeh, E.M.P., Towards an Igbo Metaphysics. Bandury, UK, Minuteman Press, 2007.

Nze, C.B, (Ed.), Aspects of Edeh's philosophy, SV. Egbekpalu, P. Edeh's Philosophy of being: A Practical and Effective Approach, Madonna University Press, Enugu, Nigeria, 2011, vol. 1.

Chapter Two

EDEH'S PROACTIVE APPRAOCH TOWARDS THE ACTUALIZATION OF THE MILLENIUM DEVELOPMENT GOALS (Mdgs)

By
Associate Professor Eneh and Oruh Charles

INTRODUCTION

Man as the only being imbued with rationality and freedom is saddled with the responsibility of transforming the vast complex globe. The imperative of this ontological responsibility is inadvertently hinged on the fact that the existence of both man and other creatures is made or marred by the extent of man's proactive responsiveness to this call. However, the struggle to escape the ugly grip of the existential malaises that bedevil human existence has been very elusive to many parts of the world while some seem to have bettered their condition. Hence, in the face of unprecedented technological explosions and vast economic resources, extreme hunger and poverty still stare humanity on the face, high level of illiteracy is still uncontestable; wars and social unrest are still rampant, et cetera.

Sequel to the above, in the year 2000, the United Nations, in a bid to collectively address these pertinent issues for an even development, came up with eight strategic goals that have come to be known as the Millennium Development Goals billed to be accomplished in or before 2015. This paper is therefore poised to evaluate the contributions of Very Rev Fr E.M.P Edeh, C.S.Sp towards the actualization of these goals especially as it concerns poverty eradication, gender equality and human empowerment, and universal basic education. It is equally poised to demonstrate that he had started executing these projects over a decade before its declaration by the United Nations.

The Millennium Development Goals

According to Wikipedia, the Millennium Development Goals (MDGs) are eight international goals for development officially established following the Millennium Summit of the United Nations in 2000 as a result of the adoption of the United Nations Millennium Declaration in which the MDGs were established. All the 193 member states of the UN and at least 23 other international organizations have agreed to achieve these goals by 2015.

The then UN Secretary General Kofi Anan set the stage for the MDGs in his famous paper, *We the Peoples: The Role of the United Nations in the Twenty-First Century*, published in 2000. The Millennium Forum made additional contributions to forming the MDGs in collaboration with more than one thousand NGOs and civil organizations across the globe.

In a nutshell, the Millennium Declaration asserts that every human being has the right to fundamental human conditions, including freedom, dignity, equality, shelter, and food. Thus "this declaration reaffirms collective values, including equality, mutual respect and shared responsibility for the conditions of all people. We must recognize that good documents and strategies alone are never enough to reduce poverty. To tackle the problem concrete actions are necessary" (Ugorji, 2009, 59–60). The MDGs, with a fifteen-year timeline for their achievement, were intended as a concrete action plan to include the following goals:

Eradication of extreme poverty and hunger
Achievement of universal primary education
Promotion of gender equality and empowerment of women
Reduction of child mortality rates
Improvement on maternal health
Combating HIV/AIDS, malaria, and other diseases
Ensuring environmental sustainability
Development of a global partnership for development

Each of the MDGs has a specific target and deadline for achieving it. Developed countries were to partner with developing countries for the realization of the goals and to facilitate this, the G8 finance ministers agreed in June 2005 to raise funds from the World Bank, the IMF, African Development Bank (AfDB) and to cancel the debts owed by the heavily indebted poor countries (HIPCs). With their debts canceled, the HIPCs could redirect that money to the goals of poverty alleviation, expansion of education and the improvement of health.

The cancellation of these debts that developing countries owed highly industrialized countries was significant, for such a debt is usually a threat to countries' development thereby rendering the plight of the indebted countries equivalent to neocolonialism. Such debts continue to widen the gap between poor and super-rich countries and if the world does not take drastic measures to reverse this trend, the gap will only widen further, leaving poor countries perpetually on the margin. Ugorji (2009) emphasizes the efforts of Pope John Paul II and other religious leaders to solicit for an extreme reduction or complete cancellation of the international debt burden to ensure equality between countries, to promote economic growth of poor countries and to restore the dignity and equality of all people in the new millennium.

Many government agencies have pledged their support toward the realization of the MDGs. In fact, most governments in Africa now provide for the accomplishment of the MDGs and international campaigns such as the UN Millennium Campaign and the Global

Poverty Project have been formed to assist in the realization of the goals. The important question remains: to what extent have these efforts yielded the desired result?

However, there is much debate surrounding both the progress towards the goals and their attainability in general. One of the major points which analysts critical of the goals are saying is that progress is uneven. A major aim of the goals is to improve the social and economic conditions of the world's poorest countries, but some critics are of the view that the goals were set despite a lack of clear analysis of them. With a good part of the aid from developed countries going to debt relief, natural disaster relief, and military aid, one wonders what developmental impact such assistance could practically make. This also leads to an important question: to what extent have the goals actually been achieved?

Edeh: A Model of Poverty Eradication

An old saying goes that a hungry man is an angry man. No human being can survive without food and we need to nourish ourselves to maintain physical and spiritual equilibrium. Today, it is impossible to build an ideal nation without a good policy to tackle the problem of poverty and its related hazards. All components of nation building are useless if they do not work to eliminate hunger and poverty. This is why the United Nations set the elimination of extreme hunger and poverty as the first of the MDGs.

Fr Edeh understands poverty very well. He knows that without food, *mmadi* suffers and becomes vulnerable to all kinds of biological and socials vices. He also knows very well that the spiritual health cannot be achieved in isolation of physical and material needs, since man is made up of both matter and soul. The harmonization of thought with action, a key feature of African philosophy, is a driving force in Edeh's zeal to arrest hunger and poverty. In this vein, Fr Edeh has established some schemes aimed at helping people earn a decent living and thus alleviate poverty and hunger:

Job Creation

A popular adage says that when you give a man a fish, he will eat for a day, but when you teach him how to fish, he will eat forever. Edeh believes that the best form of empowerment is to teach people how to permanently fend for themselves by creating employment opportunities for them. His organizations have given jobs ranging from unskilled to professional work to thousands of people in Nigeria and beyond.

Employment in Academic Institutions (Education Employment)

Onyewuenyi (2011) remarks that Edeh has more than twenty-two educational institutions at all levels throughout Nigeria. Obviously, these institutions are involved with human capital empowerment. Fr Edeh's nursery, primary, secondary, and tertiary educational institutions directly employ thousands of people and indirectly alleviate the plight of thousands more. The problem of unemployment has led youths to engage in thuggery, armed robbery, hired killing, terrorism, and other social vices and it also leads to societal moral decadence, for an idle man is the devil's workshop.

Through these institutions, Edeh provides education, a basic instrument for the destruction of social cancer and creates employment for thousands of people, both from Nigeria and abroad. Future generations of Nigeria and other nationals who could have probably turned into social parasites are now empowered to participate in mainstream economic life and by empowering them, Fr Edeh continues to bring peace to the world. The Vice Chancellor of Caritas University Amorji-Nike, Enugu, Prof Lawrence Onukwube gives us a tip of the iceberg when he states, "In Caritas University alone, Edeh provided jobs to over 600 people. In doing so, he has reduced the number of potential criminals by that number, thus bringing peace to the world" (2012, 93).

Onukwube's insight gives us a clue to the extent Edeh has gone to provide some people with a good sense of livelihood. Madonna University is twice the size of Caritas, with reference to the number of students and staff. Added to this are the staff and students of OSISATECH College of Education, OSISATECH polytechnic and the other numerous secondary and primary schools Edeh has estaestablished.

It is noteworthy that Fr Edeh does not discriminate in his hiring. Onyewuenyi (2011a) observes that Fr Edeh has over 25,800 people on his payroll across his establishments both big and small. In all his establishments, women have always been given equal opportunities as their male counterparts. Prof Onyewuenyi who is the Deputy Vice Chancellor of Caritas University, affirms that 51.9 percent of that institution's labor force are male while 48.1 percent are female, showing us that Fr Edeh is conscious of gender equality and thus strategically battles hunger and poverty through education employment.

Employment in the Health Sector

Fr Edeh has created many employment opportunities in the health sector as a means of combating hunger and poverty. In the Madonna University Teaching Hospital and in his other hospitals, including maternity hospitals, clinics, science laboratories and paramedical establishments, many people earn a livelihood for themselves and for their families. Poverty is multi-dimensional and multi-contextual and that is why even when a medical doctor, nurse or laboratory technician is jobless, such a fellow is notwithstanding vulnerable to poverty.

In fact, when people lack the opportunity to better their lives and take care of their families, they easily fall below the poverty line and when a person is severely deprived of the fundamental human needs like food, shelter, water, education, and medical care, that person is poor. In addition, when a person is unable to effectively participate in society because he or she is underemployed, that person could become psychologically poor. For instance, a medical doctor who must work as a bricklayer as a result of lack of employment opportunities in his field could be poor in this way. Therefore, Edeh has provided opportunities for medical and paramedical experts to practice their profession and to enable them live dignified and happy lives.

Provision of Mini-Industries and Self-Help Projects as Antidote to Hunger and Poverty

As we would recall, Edeh's Philosophy of Thought and Action (*EPTAism*) goes beyond philosophical speculation and indicates that man needs to be engaged productively for a meaningful survival. Because people need concrete means of living, Edeh's philosophy led him to establish mini-industries in order to create jobs and obliterate hunger and poverty. These empowerment devices include some of the following industries:

> Mini factory for the production of clean table water in Elele
> Mini factory for the production of clean table water in Okija
> Mini factory for the production of clean table water in Amorji-Nike, Enugu
> Bakery and confectionary mini-industry in Elele
> Beverage mini-industry in Elele
> Cosmetics mini-industry in Elele
> Paint factory in Elele
> Toilet tissue factory in Elele
> Wine factory in Elele

Everyone knows that the problem of unemployment is more than a mere academic exercise and Edeh's action goes the extra mile to solve it by providing jobs in these mini-industries for the betterment of *mmadi* and to put end to hunger and extreme poverty. People also learn new crafts in these mini-industries and centers, then go out on the acquisition of the requisite skills and know-how to establish their own individual businesses, thus further increasing economic opportunity.

Considering the whole chain of production from the acquisition of raw materials to the sale of finished products to the consumer, an enormous number of people's lives are touched daily by Fr Edeh through these projects. Lady Maria Gorett Omeogo of Mayfresh Savings and Loans Bank says of the project: "Hundreds of people after training have established their own businesses and are today employers of labour. Such practical economic empowerment has brought hope, peace and general well-being to the beneficiaries and the Nigerian society at large" (Omeogo. 2009, 103).

Employment in the Service Industry

Edeh's quest to exterminate hunger and poverty knows no bounds. With determination, his philosophy of charity has led him to institute the following media and service establishments and thus created many professional jobs:

> Caritas University Radio in Enugu
> Madonna University Radio in Okija, Anambra State
> Pilgrim International Newspaper
> OHHA Micro Finance Bank
> Our Saviour Printing Press, Agbani Road, Enugu

Caritas Radio is an employer of labour and also a voice of moral education and academic excellence for the society. The same is also true of Madonna University Radio, Okija. They are radio stations with a difference. In addition, they inspire morality and propagate the message of love, hope, brotherhood, proper citizenship, and of course, the philosophy of charity and peace which their founder, Emmanuel Edeh, has lived for all his life.

OHHA Bank also has many workers on its payroll from unskilled cleaners to top bank managers. At Our Saviour Printing Press many people have jobs that enable them to be financially independent, thereby overcoming the menace of poverty.

Employment in the Catholic Prayer Ministry

It is no longer news that the site of the Catholic Prayer Ministry, founded by Fr Edeh in 1985, is today a National Pilgrimage Center (National Shrine). Its elevation to this status by the papal nuncio to Nigeria in November 2012 was an epoch-making event. The National Pilgrimage Center of Eucharistic Adoration and Special Marian Devotion, Elele is the fifth largest Catholic Pilgrimage Center in the world and the first in Africa. Thousands of people go there on a daily basis to worship and to pray to God for their needs. God has blessed many people through this ministry and testimonies of miracles abound there. The ministry also employs a lot of people, including cleaners, clerks, secretaries, curators (in the museum), security guards, sales-people, and shop attendants, etc.

Poverty Eradication through Educational Empowerment

While we observe that Edeh employs a lot of people in his education establishments and thus raises their living standards, his efforts to combat hunger and poverty through education do not end there. He also uses the education itself to uproot hunger and misery from the lives of his students and graduates. To live in this modern age without proper formal education is to live without access to vast opportunities. It is difficult to imagine what life must be like, in this age of technological advancement for a youth who for instance has no rudimentary knowledge of computer.

Through education, Edeh has empowered and continues to empower thousands of youths, thereby extricating them from the brink of penury and removing the chains of hardship from them. In Edeh's schools, students acquire professional knowledge and skills that will enable them to enter the labor market upon graduation. The courses offered in these schools include but not limited to the humanities and law, nursing, medicine, laboratory science technology, food science technology, natural sciences, engineering and theology. Graduates from Edeh's institutions excel in various sectors and different countries of the world where they work and by so doing, they become asset to the Nigerian nation and global community.

Edeh is convinced that through education and compassionate care, peace is instilled in people's hearts and that if the rest of the modern world could absorb this philosophy of compassionate caring, then rancor, restiveness, kidnapping, murder, and of course hunger and poverty would be things of the past as peace would reign in the human heart and society.

The famous slogan for Nigeria, "Good People, Great Nation," is fantastic, but it is a mere fantasy if citizens, especially young citizens, are not empowered with an education that would enable them to realize their potentials. Poverty cannot be eradicated through almsgiving alone. Hunger cannot be annihilated if youths are not trained so that they could unlock the latent greatness in them. In a nation without good education, life is like the Hobbesian state of nature—solitary, poor, nasty, brutish, and short. But just as important, education without morals is like empowerment without moderation. In Edeh's institutions, education is ornamented with morals, which leads to a balanced *mmadi* and desirable citizenship. With this feature, there is always increased demand for his graduates.

Provision of Scholarships

As a way of practicing *EPTAism*, Edeh has given scholarships to various categories of students to enable them graduate and live a happy life permanently above the poverty line. Edeh believes in hard work and he encourages excellence. He is convinced that it is a sin if children and youths are not motivated to virtue, diligence, hard work, and greatness. To this end, his schools offer scholarships to students who show outstanding academic performance.

We recall that Edeh's notion of humans as *mmadi*, "good that is," derives from his creator and he is therefore permanently good because of this divine origin. In this understanding, anything that does not aid the full manifestation of his true nature is abhorrent and anti-*omenani*. Also, in this African concept of humans, it is an abomination to think of abandoning handicapped people, for to do so is to deny an authentic person of his or her authentic nature. Thus, as a way of giving them a sense of what they are, *mmadi*, Edeh created a special scholarship to enable them study and to empower them to bid adieu to extreme hunger and poverty. Many of such people have graduated from OSISATECH polytechnic and are now the breadwinners of their families.

Edeh also offers scholarships to other students in difficult circumstances. Among his students are those who encountered financial constraints and thought they would have to abandon their studies before graduation. However, Fr Founder, as he is popularly called, awards bright and disciplined students scholarships so that they do not have to leave because they cannot afford the school fees. Parents appeal to him when it seems impossible for their children to continue with their studies and in his large heart, coupled with his notion of charity and the feeling of moral responsibility towards these students, Fr Edeh usually offsets the school fees of students whose financial woes are genuine.

Work-Study Opportunity

Sound morals demand that workers should have the opportunity to grow and employees are therefore truly empowered when, in addition to a good job and salary, their employers give them opportunities to develop professionally. Fr Edeh has always encouraged his staff to further their studies while they work and a good number of his staff members have acquired higher academic degrees while they work.

Many who came into their employment in Edeh's institutions with diplomas now have first degrees, those who had first degree can now boast of having master's degrees and some of the tutorial staff who started with master's degrees even hold doctorates today. To facilitate this advancement, his workers are given easier admission to Edeh's universities and polytechnics than others. Through this practice, Edeh, in an indirect way, further empowers his employees and saves them from the menace of poverty.

Edeh also offers a work-study program for those students whose parents or guardians cannot afford the school fees. Onyewuenyi (2011) says that such students work within the institution and receive wages for their services, enabling them to defray the full cost of their education. Thus, Edeh gives them the opportunity to continue with their education and have a brighter future.

Empowerment to Host Communities of Edeh's Establishments (Corporate Social Responsibility)

Every great organization should attract development to the community in which it is established and Edeh is fully aware of this corporate social responsibility. In fact, as a way of empowering the communities where his establishments are located, he gives their local youths scholarships. His schools themselves also attract infrastructural development to the communities. Some of these communities have enjoyed roads with good access only since Edeh's institutions came there. For example, the village of Elele was relatively unknown, but thanks to Edeh's work, Elele has become a household name in Nigeria today. The presence of such institutions usually leads to the opening of various business enterprises by mainly the indigenes of the host communities around the institutions.

Empowerment through Job Security

Every worker dreams of a permanent job. To ensure job security in Fr Edeh's institutions, he believes strongly in providing equal employment opportunities and hiring on merit—he conducts key interviews himself and assesses the interviewees without discrimination. When they are hired, most members of Edeh's staff are employed permanently. It is then up to them whether they wish to continue work or to resign if they so desire. With such job security, these staff members are empowered both materially and psychologically.

Empowerment of Those in Umuogbenye (Poorest of the Poor) Rehabilitation Center

No individual has the capacity to employ all the job seekers in any country. Either because of laziness, natural or man-made circumstances, some people cannot fend for themselves. Some of these people end up as loafers and wanderers. Due to such ugly circumstances, they can neither afford shelter nor feed themselves. Many of them have neither a basic education nor knowledge of a craft. They are a liability to both their families and the state. Fr Edeh still considers them as his fellows and as *mmadi*, who still desire love, care, food, and shelter. On the premises of the Catholic Prayer Ministry in Elele is a large neighborhood called Umuogbenye (poorest of the poor) Quarters, where Edeh harbors these poor people of God. He accommodates these hundreds of people, providing food, shelter, access to medical care, and even rehabilitative services for them.

As far back as 1986, Fr Edeh established Our Saviour Rehabilitation Center in Elele for the reorientation and reintegration into society of youths who had posed danger to the society. In this way, Edeh succeeds in disentangling the poorest of the poor from the disaster of hunger and consequently converting them to valuable members of society. Without doubt, poverty is one of the causes of social vices such as armed robbery, juvenile delinquency, ethnic tension and war. Hunger and poverty also damage individuals' health. Therefore, poverty also keeps people from realizing their life goals and prevents all people from achieving peace. The UN's efforts to reduce extreme hunger and poverty therefore require the participation of everyone. In the paper *Restoring the Dignity of the Poor in Nigeria through the Millennium Development Goals*, during the theological convention at the Pilgrimage Center Elele, Nigeria, the Catholic Bishop of Umuahia, Ugorji says: "If peace is to be sustainable in Africa, there is the need to address the high incidence of poverty which insults the dignity of the human person in the continent and reduces millions of people to a life of untold hardship and undeserved misery" (Ugorji, 2009, 57).

The Millennium Development Goals Report 2012 shows that the United Nations has made progress toward MDG Number 1: Eradication of Extreme Hunger and Poverty. However, the progress does not mean that there are not also challenges. In the report, UN Secretary General Ban Ki-Moon emphasizes that the target of reducing extreme poverty by half has been reached, ahead of the 2015 deadline, and that the problem of global shelter has improved commensurately.

In line with these affirmations, the UN Undersecretary General for Economic and Social Affairs Sha Zukang confirms the Secretary General's standpoint, as he also states that there is a clear reduction of poverty in all of the world, including sub-Saharan Africa. The report further notes that the world has met the MDGs target of accessibility to clean drinking water. In addition, it points out a remarkable improvement in the lives of the world's millions of slum dwellers, even ahead of the 2020 deadline for that goal. All of these mean that the problem of reducing hunger and poverty has been reasonably addressed within the ambit of the MDGs (http://mdgs.un.org/unsd/mdg/Resources/Static/Products/Progress2012/English2012.pdf, pp. 3-5).

Evaluation

The MDGs 2012 Report actually demonstrates that the world really made progress towards MDGs Number 1: Eradication of Extreme Poverty and Hunger. However, the exercise is still not without its challenges. Although these results validate the modus operandi of the MDGs, the UN should not relax, since the whole exercise is a continuing process.

In the report, Ki-Moon also remarks that based on projections, in 2015, more than six hundred million people worldwide will still be using unimproved water sources, while almost one billion will be living on an income of less than $1.25 per day. He also notes that the menace of hunger is still not over. Undersecretary General Zukang adds that inequality adversely affects efforts toward the MDGs. He reiterates that achievement of MDG on the Eradication of Extreme Hunger and Poverty is unevenly distributed across regions and countries of the world (UN MDGs Report, 2012).

To this end, Egbutah (2009) sees agriculture, the foundation of food production, as the pillar of the effort of MDGs Number 1: Eradication of Extreme Hunger and Poverty. He makes it clear, however, that the actualization of this goal would meet a brick wall unless authorities intensified efforts to increase food production. In this way, we may also make efforts to increase food security, the accessibility to enough food and healthy nutrition for all people at all times so that they may live an active, healthy and worth life.

This is in line with the affirmation that "the most effective strategy for making steady, sustainable progress towards the MDGs by 2015 is to stimulate the interests of younger generation in agriculture by emphasizing more dynamic, functional, and practical methods in the teaching of agricultural science at all levels of our education" (Longshal and Usman, 2009, 36).

Hunger remains a worldwide challenge that surely hinders both personal and societal growth. In the case of Nigeria, Egbutah further describes the relationship between agriculture and food security thus:

"The revitalization of the agricultural sector is very essential, if the economy is to be brought back on track. This is because agriculture when properly practiced and supported has the capacity to achieve the objective of food security. To this effect, all stake holders should put their hands on the deck to ensure that the problem of food security is greatly minimized, if not eradicated. Government is advised to provide good governance and demonstrate her political will, by injecting adequate funds and providing the enabling environment for food production and food security to thrive" (Egbutah, 2009, 27).

The MDGs 2012 Report relates in addition that those in vulnerable employment have decreased, although it emphasizes that the reduction is only marginal (UN, 2012). The danger here is that those who fall in this category may resort to social deviances since they are unpaid or underpaid for their labour. This is a critical challenge which needs to be addressed in order to avoid among others, the exploitation of workers by their employees.

Recommendations from *EPTAism*

The Philosophy of *Mmadi*: Understanding the true nature of humans as "good that is" is an important step to the solution of human problems. It is when people are accepted within this context of divine origin that policy makers at the local, national, and international levels will make effective laws and policies that improve human welfare.

Continuous Job Creation: Edeh continuously creates jobs as a weapon for combating poverty and hunger, and he continues to explore available avenues in which he can invest to create more jobs for families, thus putting an end to their hardship. The MDGs should likewise be focused on the angle of job creation because without the continuous creation of employment, the problems of poverty and hunger would continue and the MDGs Number 1 would continue to suffer a setback.

Continuous Provision of Good Drinking Water: Water is a necessity for human existence and Fr Edeh is fully aware of this. This is why he has strategically embarked on projects to produce clean drinking water to serve all his organizations. However, no individual can provide water for the whole world, so the United Nations should partner with indigenous governments of the world in a bid to provide drinking water for all communities and thus prevent waterborne diseases like typhoid and cholera.

Provision of Shelter: In Edeh's institutions, students are entitled to full accommodation and a good number of staff members, both faculty and non-faculty, are also given accommodation in Elele, Okija, and Akpugo, etc. Edeh believes that any human being without shelter is already poor, so he provides accommodation in order to create an enabling environment for his staff and their families.

Incentive to the Disabled (deaf, mute, blind, and handicapped): These people have no voice in the MDGs Report 2012, so we do not know to what extent the United Nations has developed a specific work plan to accommodate them in our society. Can the MDGs Number 1 be said to have genuinely made progress when this group is not particularly considered? In this regard, the UN can learn from Fr Edeh, who has an action plan for the integration of disabled people into the society for the benefit of all. As already mentioned, he provides a scholarship for them at OSISATECH polytechnic and he engages them by giving them the opportunity to learn crafts at his mini-industries and other employment schemes.

Commitment to Employment on Merit: Many people today are poor not necessarily because they cannot work but because they are victims of discrimination. *Mmadi* in Edeh means that all in the human community are the same. When people are discriminated against, they get frustrated and dejected and can become antisocial.

Poverty as a result of racism, nepotism, tribalism, and gender inequality are all evil in the sight of the Creator, Chineke. The United Nations should also consider how to address this type of poverty caused by unnecessary discriminations in the society. Edeh sets standard for different categories of workers irrespective of where they come from. Nobody is denied access to opportunities in his organization as a result of racism or favoritism. To do so, the MDGs could be structured to encourage parity in opportunities, in different sectors all over the world; coupled with hiring based on merit, as evident in Edeh's methods.

Edeh: A Model of Education for All

Academic Institutions founded by Edeh:

Madonna University, Okija, Nigeria (1999)—the first private university
in Nigeria and the first Catholic university in West Africa
Caritas University, Amorji-Nike, Enugu (2004)
OSISATECH Polytechnic, Enugu (1989)—the first private polytechnic
in Nigeria
OSISATECH College of Education, Enugu (1989) -the first private
College of Education in Nigeria
Saviourite House of Foramtion (Senior Seminary), Enugu
5 secondary schools
3 primary schools
3 nursery schools (kindergartens)

Scholarship Programs at Edeh's Institutions:

Scholarship program for the handicapped
Work-study program
Scholarship for academic excellence
Scholarship for indigent youth
Special scholarship programme for the physically challenged
Special scholarship program for host communities

Scholarly Publications (Books) by Fr Prof. Edeh
Towards an Igbo Metaphysics, 1985. Translated into Italian, Spanish, French,
and the Igbo language.
Peace to the Modern World, 2006.
Igbo *Metaphysics: The First Articulation of African Philosophy of Being*,
2009.
Authentic Catholic Theology, 2008.
Edeh's Charity Peace Model, 2012.
The New Philosophy: At the Service of Truth, 2011.
University Cooperation: Experiences in Founding Catholic Universities, 2011.

Qualitative Catholic Education as the Basis for Meaningful Development as Evident from Blessed Pope John Paul II's Proposals, 1995–2005, 2011.

Publications Edited by Prof. Edeh

The Church of Jesus the Saviour in Africa, Vol. 1 (Lineamenta), 2009. Organizer and editor.

The Church of Jesus the Saviour in Africa, Vol. 2 (Instrumentum Laboris), 2009. Organizer and editor.

The Catholic Prayer Ministry and the Pilgrimage Center of Eucharistic Adoration and Special Marian Devotion, Elele, 2004.

Madonna University: An Institution with a Difference, 2004.

God the Father the Beginning and End: Tertio Millennio, Vol. 2, 2008.

Jesus the Saviour in Our Midst: The Third Millennium, Vol. 1, 1998.

The Holy Spirit Acting in Our Midst: The Third Millennium, Vol.2, 2000.

The Pilgrimage Center of Eucharistic Aaristi Adoration, 1997. Edited with I. K. B. Ngwoke.

Some of the Scholarly Books Published Exclusively about Edeh

The Mustard Seed of Jesus the Saviour in Elele, by R. N Onyewuenyi,.

Authentic Human Development: Insights from the Metaphysics of Rev Fr Prof. Edeh, edited by Onyema Uzoamaka, 2009.

African Philosophy: Contemporary Trends, edited by Stephen Ojobor, 2009.

Aspects of Edeh's Philosophy, Vol. 1, edited by C. B. Nze, 2011.

Aspects of Edeh's Philosophy, Vol. 2, edited by Ezechi Chukwu, 2011.

Actualization of the Millennium Development Goals: Fr Edeh as a Pacesetter, edited by Ezechi Chukwu, 2013.

Edeh's Charity Peace Model (ECPM) First and Second Editions. Edited by N. N. Chukwuemeka, 2012.

Fr Emmanuel M.P. Edeh: Inspiring 21ˢᵗ Century Africans to Serve First, by P. Amah, 2012.

The Dignity of Man in African Metaphysics as Epitomized in EPTAism, by M. Melladu, 2011.

Servant-Leader Emmanuel M.P. Edeh: An Inspiration in Youth Empowerment & Poverty Alleviation: The Nigerian Experience, by R. N. Onyewuenyi, 2011.

Peace to the Modern Society: A Short History of the Father Founder Very Rev Prof. E.M.P Edeh CSSp. 2004, by Mother John Bosco Kalu, SJS

Fr Edeh Before the Journalists. Editor Barr. Emeka Okpala, 2011 Responses to the Questionnaire on Very Rev Fr Prof. Emmanuel Mathew Paul Edeh CSSp, OFR Editor Rev Sr Dr Purissima Egbekpalu SJS, 2011

A Short Profile of Very Rev Fr Prof. Emmanuel M.P Edeh CSSp, OFR, 2010, By Albert U. Ogbodo PhD

A Short Biography of Very Rev Fr Prof. Emmanuel M.P Edeh CSSP. OFR, 2011 By Zulu Adigwe

Biodata of a Legend of our Time, Very Rev Fr Prof. Emmanuel Mathew, Rev Paul Edeh CSSp., OFR by Fr JoJosephat Emeka Ezenwajiaku FJS, 2011.

Man and Peace in the light of Edeh Philosophy of thought and Action, by Assoc. Prof. Remy Onyewuenyi CSSp, PhD, 2012

Edeh has founded educational institutions to better the lot of humans and in Fr Edeh the Catholic priest, there also exists Prof Edeh the teacher, scholar, researcher, and author. As a result of his amazing contributions to education and the practical improvement in the realities of human existence, students and researchers today investigate Edeh's life and espouse his thought for the benefit of the academic world and humanity at large.

The large number of papers on Edeh presented regularly in academic and religious institutions enrich the intellectual community. Furthermore, those articles, books and other publications facilitate the development of African philosophy in particular, human development and aid the cultivation of global citizenship in general. In Edeh's words: "It is obvious that when every person lives one's nature as 'good that is,' the echo of *mmadi* would transverse humanity because man sees himself in the being of others, his goodness in the goodness of others, and peace would eventually reign in the world" (personal interview with Edeh, March 2011).

The Madonna University International Convention of Experts and Intellectuals, an annual five-day rendezvous of intellectuals organized by Madonna University in Nigeria, usually attracts accomplished scholars and experts around the globe to inform participants about the life and philosophy of Edeh in general and the practical application of his philosophy in various contexts around the world. Many scholars for instance discuss his philosophy of *mmadi*, which is neither selective nor discriminatory. His pioneering work and masterpiece, *Towards an Igbo Metaphysics*, earned him an award in 2011 as an articulator of African philosophy of being from the prestigious University of Nigeria, Nsukka.

Edeh has made a landmark achievement in education. His desire is to use education in addition to academic excellence to recognize and position man genuinely as *mmadi* in all people and thus consolidate the ontological nature of human as "good that is" who is in permanent cohesion with his Creator. Edeh's academic centers, which are all founded on sound moral principles, are designed as formative institutions that respond to the material and spiritual needs of humanity, unlike most other contemporary institutions of learning, which are purely concerned with academic performance. Ebo confirms:

"It is reasonable to argue that formal education, that is the type of programmed instruction and knowledge imparted in designated centres according to conventional criteria taken in isolation, can never encompass the significant range of forces that go to the shaping of the individual personality. A complex organism, the human individual is of forces from diverse sources that incessantly impinge upon him and condition his feelings, memories and perceptions. Formal education is a major source of these formative influences. Other equally significant sources are less structured" (1989, 30).

The need to blend formal education with the "less structured" significant forces of formative influence, including the nonmaterial and the supra-temporal, led Edeh to develop a curriculum of all-round education for the comprehensive development of man. For instance, at all his tertiary academic institutions students must attend a three-hour orientation once a week that includes two hours of physical exercise and then moral instruction. Irrespective of his tight schedule, Fr Edeh dedicates time to partake in this exercise as he considers physical exercise to be an integral habit for the well- being of the students and the larger society.

The first executive president of Nigeria, Alhaji Shehu Shagari, delivered a paper titled "Education: The Greatest Investment for Development" at the convocation of Bayero University, Kano, on 16 January 16 1982, in which he said the following of education and development:

"Education must enhance political, personal, and social development. Man must be taught political awareness and knowledge of civic responsibilities. Education must ensure democratic and human ideals and an even and just distribution of resources and social amenities like schools, hospitals, shops, markets, and factories, without tying these with party politics. Education must foster and nationalism. It must produce selfless political leaders who are objective and non-tribalistic. It must allow personal development. Man must preserve his social identity by way religions, traditions, and customs; respect for one's heritage brings with it a sense of security. Science and health education must enhance the quality of human life and fight dirt, pollution, destitution, and delinquency" (Shagari, 1982, 67).

It was as if President Shehu Shagari had read the mind of Fr Emmanuel Edeh when presenting this paper, even though Edeh was in far away Chicago as a researcher. Fr Edeh returned to Nigeria two years later and since then, he has made monumental strides toward accomplishing all of the points Shagari raised in that address. From fostering poverty alleviation to education, health to youth empowerment, social justice to religion, cooperation to unity, charity to peace, Edeh has stood tall among his contemporaries. Edeh's God-man-world scheme as evident in Igbo metaphysics underpins that no society can be truly human without morality and sense of responsibility. According to Edeh (2009), this scheme gives credence to the dignity of human being and human existence.

As a way of matching words with action in the education sector, thereby affirming the *ime* (doing) part of African philosophy, Edeh began establishing institutions of learning in the mid-1980s. Edeh had the need to nurture his fellow humans as authentic *mmadi* and as world citizens at a time when education in Nigeria was almost comatose.

Life is faced with difficulties and these challenges remain as we advance both individually and collectively. However, because we are rational beings, these chokepoints should only stir us to greater efforts to improve on what we have, allowing our one talent or endowment to become two. We as individuals and our governments have a great responsibility to teach such a philosophy to youth and thus put them on the path of learning for life. Edeh believes strongly that the mind of every human being needs to be instructed and improved with education and religion.

The learning environment should promote students' growth by providing suitable support for acquiring skills and learning proper behaviour, attitudes, and values. Education is vital for the fullness of *mmadi* and the importance of the learning environment towards that goal should not be underestimated. In that regard, Edeh (2006) insists that the achievement of African philosophy, which values holistic care for all as members of one family, could not be realized without good education. Edeh recalls the devastation of the Nigerian Civil War of 1967–70, which led to the near total collapse of the educational system in the country and giving way to myriad of institutional vices like exam malpractice, campus violence, and academic decay in general (Edeh, 2006).

Consequently, thousands of helpless youths ended up as armed robbers, killing and destroying human lives and properties. It was in the face of the above circumstances that Edeh struggled from 1989 to present to establish different categories of government certified tertiary institutions for the provision of quality education and moral excellence. Today, these institutions—OSISATECH Polytechnic, OSISATECH College of Agriculture, Madonna University, and Caritas University Enugu—are all citadels of good education.

The ancient Greek pre-Socratic philosopher Heraclitus (circa 500 BC) who says that fire is the origin of all things also says that permanence is an illusion, as all things are in perpetual flux. Following this Heraclitan dictum, the founding of Edeh's tertiary educational institutions restored confidence in education in the country. Parents and guardians sent their children to his institutions where they received good education and where there is the absence of those social ailments that had previously devastated the educational system.

In order to relieve parents of the burden of school fees, especially the poor and the handicapped, Edeh instituted extensive scholarship programs in each of the institutions he founded. Dr Mike Ike Okwudili, the Rector of OSISATECH Polytechnic, testified that Edeh's institutions were established to transform Edeh's thought into reality and that Edeh has provided academic and moral education in these institutions. He stresses that Edeh's scholarship programs provide for the disabled and abjectly poor, thereby transforming the lives of many students who had been a burden to society. Dr Okwudili goes on: "Worthy of mention is the case of Agbakuribe Bamidele, a blind man who benefitted from Edeh's scholarship scheme who is now a lecturer in the University of Abuja. He is currently pursuing his Ph.D. and is happily married with children" (Okwudili, 2011, 159). Many such beneficiaries of *EPTAism* consequently add value to society.

Former Deputy Vice Chancellor of Madonna University, Okija, Associate Professor Ngwoke (2006), remarks that Fr Edeh can be summarily described as a person whose desires have been modeled through his continuous self-sacrifice for peace, reconciliation, rebuilding of shattered lives and restoration of lost hope. Since 1984, Fr Edeh has been strenuously engaged in the arduous tasks of paring his philosophy with action not only by himself but also and above all, through his educational institutions.

In his assessment of Edeh's academic institutions, Unegbu (1996), the former Vice Chancellor of Caritas University, says that Edeh established a good number of "humanistic institutions" that cater to the various needs of mankind:

"In his human development efforts, he has established Our Saviour educational system that operates at all levels: namely primary, secondary, and tertiary. His preoccupation for the welfare of the abjectly poor, the handicapped and the less privileged in the society has propelled him to establish full scholarships for any member of these groups that qualifies and gains admission into any of these levels" (2006, 75).

Unegbu (2006) further relates that in these educational institutions, Fr Edeh has set out to correct the evils and institutional anomalies that for years plagued the entirety of the Nigerian educational system and made it a source of ridicule, including secret cultism, campus unrest, strikes by staff and students, examination malpractices, imposition of the purchase of handouts on students, sorting, and sexism. In contrast, in Edeh's academic institutions, there is no room for these ills which bedevil education in Nigeria. Therefore, they are exemplary institutions.

Prof. A.U. John Kamen (2006) describes the Nigerian education industry before Edeh joined it as being in "shambles" and that "the state of education was nothing to write home about. Incessant riots and strikes among students or staff ravaged the educational system. In 1997, for instance, apart from Fr Edeh's OSISATECH Polytechnic and OSISATECH College of Education, all the tertiary institutions in the country were on strike for almost one full year" (82). It is easy to see the difference Edeh's institutions make.

Unegbu (2006) goes on to explain that through these institutions, Edeh has uplifted the abjectly poor and benefitted numerous troubled youths through his scholarship programs, thereby contributing to both human development and the betterment of society. Edeh is therefore, a reformer of education, his knowledge of *mmadi* and his inventiveness, love, dedication, and charity have enabled him to achieve monumental change in academia, thus fostering genuine peace in the world.

In addition, Ezechi Chukwu (2013) takes the stance that Edeh's institutions are dedicated to the teaching of moral values, thereby encouraging global citizenship among the students. Chukwu opines that some of these ingredients of *EPTAism* should be adopted by the United Nations for the smooth and effective implementation of the MDGs, especially in education.

The MDGs Report 2012 shows that, against all odds, some progress is evident towards achieving parity in primary education for boys and girls, with girls seeing more benefits, and improvement in sub-Saharan Africa, compared with figures before the MDGs were set. The report emphasizes that enrollment rates for children in primary schools have increased and that rates of children out of school have decreased (UN MDGs Report, 2012).

This achievement is encouraging since education is the pillar of human development and that is why it is enshrined in the MDGs. No matter a person's area of endeavour, education nurtures that person and gives him or her sense of direction in all his or her undertakings. Education equips us with skills, knowledge, and the wherewithal to optimize our potentials, be effective in our career, and fully actualize ourselves. Education is so important to human development that all countries of the world have their own policies for it.

Emphasizing the importance of education as key to the actualization of the MDGs, Mfam (2009) discusses vocational education in particular, noting that in both the private and public sectors, when employees have the right skills, obtained through the proper education, administrative efficiency is achieved, productivity improves, the economy of both the nation in question and the world definitely improve. Thus: "To achieve productive work for youth as envisaged under the MDGs, requisite industrial and employability skills and vocational competencies should be part and parcel of the learning experiences offered to students" (Mfam, 2009, 21). In addition, vocational educational programs enhance employment opportunities, entrepreneurial know-how and managerial capacity of women, who are currently behind their male counterparts in employment.

To this end, "vocational-technical education is indispensible in the attainment of MDGs" (Mfam, 2009, 22). While the achievements of the UN's goal in education is commendable, the UN is encouraged to intensify its efforts towards MDGs Number 2 and all stakeholders should collaborate to meet this goal, for education teaches not only skills and general knowledge, but it also imparts value to humans, gives them morals, and breeds good citizenship both at the local and international levels.

The aim of MDGs Number 2 should be combined with the educational aims of the United Nations' Educational, Scientific, and Cultural Organization (UNESCO), which was founded in 1946 as an autonomous and permanent intergovernmental organization and agency of the United Nations. Its primary function is to foster peace and security among nations through education, science, and culture. It also advances universal respect for justice and the rule of law, human rights and freedom for all peoples of the world. With UNESCO's help, the propagation of mutual knowledge through worthy education and the cooperation of nations could be easily realized.

Evaluation

The French thinker Maritain (1943) remarks that the teaching of morality should take fundamental position in schools. The ancient Greek philosopher Plato also believed that genuine philosophical knowledge is the knowledge of the immaterial transcendent forms that are true reality. One of the central themes of Plato's concept of knowledge and education is the benefit of acquiring knowledge for its own sake. This informs Plato's philosophy of education and sociopolitical philosophy in general which attribute the leadership of the polis to the philosopher king who has a commensurate knowledge for the administration of the body politic.

The acquisition of knowledge, whether it is in terms of military tactics or public administration, requires rigorous effort by the individual. No doubt, this commitment is worthwhile because education is an integral component of human development. This is why Plato makes a clear distinction between the Sophist and the philosopher:

"The Sophist takes refuge in the darkness of non-being, where he is at home and has the knack of feeling his way, and it is the darkness of the place that makes him so hard to perceive... Whereas the philosopher, whose thoughts constantly dwell upon the nature of reality, is difficult to see because his region is so bright, for the eye of the vulgar soul cannot endure to keep its gaze fixed on the divine (Plato, 1969, 999).

The progress towards achieving MDGs Number 2 is not smooth in every sense of the word, as the UN Under-Secretary-General for Economic and Social Affairs remarks in the MDG Report 2012 that the achievements were unequally distributed across regions and countries. A typical example of this inequality is evident between sub-Saharan Africa and Southern Asia. It is reported that in 2010, sub-Saharan Africa had 24 percent of children of primary-school age out of school and Southern Asia reported 7 percent (UN MDGs Report, 2012).

The report further notes that there is in the world generally, a reduction in girls' exclusion from primary education, but a disparity in the improvement exists between regions and countries. Further on enrolment, there is also a danger that some pupils who register for primary school may not complete their studies due to financial constraints which though vary from one region to another. The need to complete primary school also points to the need for more secondary schools, as they may not be available in some areas due to economic limitations. Poverty also makes it difficult or impossible for families to send their children to school, just as more urban children attend school than those in rural areas (UN MDGs Report, 2012).

In short, the children who cannot go to school remain disadvantaged and have a bleak future. The MDGs should be rechanneled to close these gaps in access to education. When this happens, education will lead to development. Since development is all about human enhancement and in turn, enhancement of society in general, the achievement of MDGs Number 2 must be prioritized and the world should work hard in this direction. Chibueze (2009), in citing UNESCO 2008, relates that the international resolution to meet the 2015 target on education might be unattainable due to the poor learning outcomes in languages and mathematics across the world.

Recommendations from *EPTAism*

It is undeniable that progress has been made towards the MDGs regarding education. However, a lot more needs to be done, as we have seen. To accomplish this, we can borrow some ideas from Edeh, who has made astonishing success in education.

Adoption of the concept of *mmadi*: The United Nations should consider Edeh's concept of humans as "good that is" in the formulation of its education policy. Until the world comes to realize that all humans are ontologically good as a result of their origin, it will be difficult to achieve comprehensive education. The world needs care and love and Edeh provides them before anything else to his pupils/students. His concept of charity requires them, for without care and love, discrimination, maltreatment, indifference, and social disparity will continue unabated.

Absence of Gender Discrimination: As a way of filling the gap between enrolment of male and female students, gender is not a condition for admission in any of Edeh's schools, which have given access to education to thousands of people from different parts of the world. Because of his notion of *mmadi* and his concept of charity, he has created in these institutions enabling study environments, despite the great cost it imposes on him, so that many African youths, and Nigerians in particular, may realize their dreams of having good education and a fulfilled life.

Thousands of the youths who attend Edeh's schools could have ended up on the streets had it not been for the efforts of the ordinary priest and teacher, Emmanuel Edeh. Onyewuenyi (2011a) notes that these institutions have offered education of undoubted quality to "over 53,000 youths" and this number continues to grow annually as students graduate. On the issue of gender parity in admission and educational opportunity, Onyewuenyi observes that this problem has already been solved in Edeh's institutions and that the gap has been filled already.

Of the students who matriculated in Caritas University in Enugu between 2007 and 2010, more of them were female than male. Onyewuenyi states: "Of the 2,331 who matriculated during the period, 1,195 (51.3%) are female while the remaining 1,136 (48.7%) are male. This is a change; a phenomenon to watch. It can be inferred from these figures that Fr Edeh is not just offering the youth University education but equal University education opportunity" (Onyewuenyi, 2011a, 57).

Merit as the Condition for Admission: The only condition for admission into Edeh's institutions is merit, not gender, a quota system, bribery, nepotism, or favoritism, for these illicit conditions inhibit academic progress and the optimization of human knowledge, for they discourage excellence.

The Inculcation of Moral Values to Students: Another important factor that the MDGs seem not to have considered is the moral disposition of graduates. Education is human formation and if we pay attention only to the technical aspect of academic knowledge at the expense of the moral and spiritual facets, the system would only produce mediocre citizens imbued with mechanistic and anthropocentric conception of man. This is another pillar of education in Edeh, a situation whereby formal education is blended with sound moral values.

Aid to the Less Privileged: In the MDGs Report 2012, the UN did not give the details of how the handicapped and less privileged in society have fared in education or whether any provision has been specifically made for them in the goal. However, Edeh has made a provision for them. At OSISATECH polytechnic as earlier mentioned they are offered scholarship to enable them have access to tertiary education. The UN should follow suit, otherwise handicapped people will be permanently left behind.

Quality Schools from Nursery to University: The UN should also partner with various national governments to provide quality schools for students and pupils across the globe at all levels, especially in third world countries in order to accommodate the teeming global population, following the example of Edeh, who provides good quality schools from nursery to the university level.

Completion of Academics: It is not enough for the UN to consider only the enrolment of male and female students in MDGs Number 2. Whether they finish their studies is just as important. In Nigeria for instance, industrial action by lecturers and sometimes on-campus violence by students have often led to the elongation of students' academic careers by an additional one or two years. This disheartening situation, however, does not exist in Edeh's institutions. In all of Edeh's academic institutions, courses of study always fit within the timeframe of the school calendar and students graduate by the date stipulated as the official end of their courses.

Security: Unfortunately, student cultism festers in most academic tertiary institutions in Nigeria of today. These organized criminal enterprises made up of students mastermind terror to their fellow students, lecturers, and school staff. It is not clear whether the MDGs have considered this inhibitor to education. An academic institution ought to be a citadel of knowledge and not an incubator of gangsterism. To prevent this type of activity, Edeh provides accommodation with twenty-hour security measures in all his tertiary institutions. Except during holidays, students leave campus only by permission after indicating the purpose of their exit, thus keeping students and staff safe during this period of vulnerability.

Welfare: In addition to adequate security, Edeh increases student welfare by providing clean water, electricity, recreational facilities, etc.

Religious Tolerance: The MDG Report 2012 does not indicate the extent to which the MDGs have ensured the free integration of students of divergent religious backgrounds into the academic environment. However, Edeh's institutions have a strategic lesson to teach: although they are Catholic institutions, they are also open to students and staff of other religions, as they are communities of *mmadi* and therefore do not engage in religious discrimination. Christians of different denominations are entitled to their beliefs and to worship as they wish and so are Muslims and members of other faiths.

Discipline: Another important characteristic of Edeh's institutions is the rigorous enforcement of discipline for both staff and students for the common good. Lecturers are made to attend classes at the appropriate time and to structure their courses following school ordinances and assess students' examinations objectively. Students are required to attend lectures and do their assignments and their adherence to these rules is continuously assessed. Furthermore, undisciplined activities like the viewing of obscene films and other erotic materials are completely outlawed in Edeh's institutions. Violent and unruly acts like fighting, stealing, and sabotage are met with severe punishments.

These are some of the strategies Fr Prof. Edeh successfully employs in his educational institutions that the United Nations should emulate to realize MDGs Number 2. Most parents who send their children to Edeh's schools today do so because of these innovations. Knowledge is power and the good use of it is more powerful. For the development of any nation, promotion of education must be on the front burner. Edeh's philosophy of *mmadi*, with its practical application through *EPTAism*, has transformed education in his institutions and it can be hoped that it will take the world far if it is adopted as a means to implement the MDG Number 2, especially MDGs in Africa and the third world in general.

Conclusion

The foregoing underscores the fact that Edeh has contributed immensely to the actualization of the MDGs especially in Africa. More appreciable is the fact that, in his foresight, he had, for more than a decade, started to work assiduously to wipe these dents off the face of humanity.

The dynamics of Edeh's proactive approach to the achievement of these goals issue from earlier discovery of a practical and viable philosophy— the philosophy of *mmadi*, which makes available the right understanding of man—an understanding that enkindled in him the unquenchable zeal to resuscitate his fellow human beings from their pitiable conditions of existential ills long before the United Nation's declaration of the MDGs. It could therefore be averred that while the various nations of the world were woken up to this tasks by this official declaration, Edeh was far earlier inspired to it by his discovery of African philosophy of *mmadi*.

REFERENCES

Chibueze, O.G 2009. "Improvisation and utilization of infrastructural materials in primary English Pedagogy: A key to achieving the millennium development goals Nigeria by 2015." The voice of teachers, teachers without borders, Africa Regional chapter, Abuja 1(1).

Ebo, C.1989. "Formal Education British and America alternatives." In azikwe and African revolution, edited by M.S.O. Olisa and Ikejiane clark. Ibadan: Africana-FEP Publishers

------. 2006. *Peace to the Modern World: A Way Forward Through the Concrete Living of the Existential Dictates of the African Philosophy of Being.* Banbury, UK: Minuteman Press.

-------. 2009. *Igbo Metaphysics: The First Articulation of African Philosophy of Being.* Enugu: Madonna University Publications

Eghutah, E.U. 2009. "Food Security in Nigeria: Concept and Strategies for Improvement." The voice of teachers, teachers without borders, Africa regional chapter, abuja1 (1).

Kanem, J.A.U. 2006 "Testimony by prof. A. U. John Kanem." In peace to the modern world: a way forward through the concrete living of the existential dictates of the African philosophy of being. Banbury, UK: Minuteman press.

Longshal, M. W., and M. Usman. 2009. "Achieving the millennium development goals (MDGs) by 2015 through effective teaching of agricultural science in Nigeria." The voice of teachers, teachers without borders, African regional chapter. Abuja1 (1).

Maritain, Jacques. 1943. *Education at the Crossroads.* New Haven. Yale University Press.

Mfam, K. I. 2009. "Vocational and technical education: a panacea for achieving the millennium development goals in Nigeria." The voice of teachers, teachers without borders. African regional chapter. Abuja 1 (1).

Ngwoke, Bernard. 2006. "Testimony by Very Rev Fr Assoc Prof Bernard IK Ngwoke." In *Peace to the Modern World: A Way Forward through the Concrete Living of the Existential Dictates of the African Philosophy of Being.* Banbury: UK: Minuteman Press.

Okwudile, Mike Ike. 2011. "Education from Edeh's philosophy of thought and action (*EPTAism*)." In *Aspects of Edeh's Philosophy, Vol. 2,* edited by Chukwu Ezechi. Enugu: Madonna University Press.

Omeogo, M. G. 2009. "Jobs for the jobless in the life of Fr Edeh." In *Authentic Human Development: Insights from the Metaphyisics of Rev Fr Prof. Edeh*, edited by Onyema Uzoamaka. Enugu: Madonna University Press.

Onukwube, Lawrence C. 2012. "The establishment of Caritas University in Enugu: Motivation and expectation towards peace." In *Man and Peace: In the Light of Edeh's Philosophy of Thought and Action (EPTAism)*, edited by R. Onyewuenyi. Enugu: Madonna University Press.

-------. 2011a. *In Aspects of Edeh's Philosophy, Vol. 2,* edited by Ezechi Chukwu. Enugu: Madonna University Press.

Plato. 1969. *The Collected Dialogues of Plato*. Edited by Edith Hamilton and Huntington Cairns. Bollingen Series LXXI. New York: Pantheon.

Shagari, Shehu. 1982. "Education: the greatest investment for development." In *The Challenge of Change: Collected Speeches of President Shehu Shagari, Vol.3*. Lagos: Federal Department of Information, Domestic Publicity Division.

Ugorji, Lucius Iwejuru. 2009. "Restoring the dignity of the poor in Nigeria through the millennium development goals." In The *Church of Jesus the Savior Africa, Vol. 1 (Lineamenta)*, organized and edited by E.M.P. Edeh. Enugu: Madonna University Press.

Unegbu, R.O. 2006. "Testimony by Prof R. O. Unegbu." In *Peace to the Modern World: A Way Forward through the Concrete Living of the Existential Dictates of the African Philosophy of Being*. Banbury, UK: Minuteman Press.

Chapter Three

EDEH AND THE U.N. MELLENIUM DEVELOPMENT GOALS

Isaac Nginga & Oliver Onyeka Ugwu

INTRODUCTION

The question of man and his existence have been a perennial one. In his nature, man loathes suffering, and thrives well in environment of peace and comfort, but he is inclined also to conflict and evil. Thus, the life of man has been that of struggle against self, or to conquer self, nature and his environment including his fellow for his good life and peace. This explains why man has been described severally as *homo rationalis, homo sapiens, homo fabar, homo politicus, homo lipus,* and what have you. In the course of human civilization, man has explored and exploited self and his environment to make life worth living but regrettably his life has been predominantly colored by misery, war, pain, emptiness, and death.

At the wake of the First and Second World Wars, the most horrible and devastating experiences of man in the modern world, the League of Nations, turned into United Nations came together to have common front in challenging the human common enemies suffering, misery, and war. In its landmark summit, the Millennium Summit, 2000, the United Nation came up with a draft program called Millennium

Development Goals (MDGs) aimed at ending man's misery and fostering global development and partnership in 2015. The 8-point United Nation agenda called Millennium Development Goals are:

1) Eradicating extreme poverty and hunger
2) Achieving universal primary education
3) Promoting gender equality and empowering women
4) Reducing child mortality rates
5) Improving maternal health
6) Combating HIV/AIDS, malaria, and other diseases
7) Ensuring environmental sustainability
8) Developing a global partnership for development

Each of the goals has specific stated targets and dates for achieving those targets. To accelerate progress, "the G8 Finance Ministers agreed in June 2005 to provide enough funds to the World Bank, the International Monetary Fund (IMF), and the African Development Bank (ADB)" to cancel some debt owed by members of the heavily indebted poor countries to allow poor countries to re-channel the resources saved from the forgiven debt to social programs for improving health and education and for alleviating poverty.

Progress towards reaching the goals has been potholed by some factors that militate against them. Some countries have achieved many of the goals, while others seem not to be on the track to realize any. A United Nation conference in September 2010 reviewed progress and concluded with the adoption of a global action plan to achieve the eight anti-poverty goals by the 2015 targeted date. There are also new commitments on women's and children's health and new initiatives globally against poverty, hunger, and disease. Hence, the concerns of the MDGs are to encourage development by improving social and economic conditions in the world towards reduction of poverty to its minimum and for a healthier international cooperation.

Philosophers, sociologists, economists, political theorists have in the course of human civilization espoused ideas that will better man and the human society. Important point to make here is that as much as one may agree that a well-thought idea or philosophy may be workable or effective either in the short or long term not all are life-giving, life "generating" and sustaining. Some are destructing and anti-human. Edeh's philosophy, articulated in his classic work Towards an Igbo Metaphysics, 1985, is indeed a philosophy of life and development. One can rightly say that Edeh's philosophy of *mmadi* the basis for Edeh's Philosophy of Thought and Action is indeed the thought behind the UN's Millennium Development Goals. In his proactivity and ingenuity, Edeh has, close to two decades before the UN's Millennium Summit, 2000 offered the world a philosophy of life, development and partnership; and has in reality strategically been working to actualizing such lofty ideals of the United Nations.

This chapter presents to you both a blend of Edeh's philosophy and the aspirations of Millennium Development Goals and in particular, Edeh's personal contributions to the realization of MDGs. It will also reveal or expose some challenges and basic lapses not put into consideration by UN in the draft and so militate against the workability of the MDGs. Edeh, on the other hand, provides us handy such salient elements which form and are indeed the principles that drive his veritable approach in the realization of the MDGs. Our concentration here is on the last five goals.

Edeh and Sustainable Healthcare Delivery

Health is wealth, for an unhealthy person cannot perform optimally. Edeh's 2006 book, Peace to the Modern World has two major semantic purposes: first, to provide Fr Edeh's declaration to serve humanity and second, to give testimony of the concrete and self-evident practicality of that declaration. In that piece, Edeh posits his mission of practical and effective charity, reiterating his commitment to care for all the people of God, including the insane, needy, sick, and downtrodden.

As part of his mission to instill peace in humanity, Fr Edeh established the public healthcare delivery schemes listed above to cater to the health needs of *mmadi*. Edeh states, "For the healthcare of the abjectly poor and abandoned it became imperative to found a number of medical institutions to bring healthcare to the doorsteps of the thousands in the society who cannot help themselves" (2006, 11). These initiatives demonstrate the immense value Fr Edeh assigns to human life, which is no surprise in light of his notion of humans as "good that is." Edeh does not want to leave any category of *mmadi* without proper care and love and he always desires to bring peace to everyone, therefore he has founded the various healthcare delivery schemes listed above, for he knows that ill-health strips human potential as well as human life.

Amah (2012) states that Edeh is convinced that people's intrinsic potentials, if harnessed properly, will enable them to rise above their limitations. Edeh therefore maximizes everything within his reach to lift people from the shackles of ill-health and empower them to bring about the best of themselves. To accomplish this, he spends time in consultation with those who bring their multifarious needs to him. He does not allow them to go unless he has given them the attention, care, and love that they deserve. Since God, *Osebuluwa*, cares for man, Edeh believes that we should care for *mmadi* by showing all love and providing for their good health. Peter Amah summarizes Fr Edeh's efforts thus:

"From my interviews and observations, it appears Edeh is not necessarily the voice of the voiceless as much as he is, on a small scale, the food to the hungry, clothes to the naked, home to the homeless, healing to the sick, hope for the hopeless, courage to the weary, shelter to the orphans, peace to those in conflict. He plays these and many other virtuous roles, sometimes on a large scale, because of his faith in and desire to emulate Jesus the Saviour. He is man with goals who is giving, humble, and result-oriented" (2012, 33).

Edeh is committed to the healing of all sicknesses, both physical and spiritual. As Amah's interviews reveal, Edeh plays out his "virtuous roles" on a large scale because of his faith in Jesus the Savior and his passionate desire to emulate him.

Edeh's healthcare initiatives began with the establishment of Our Saviour Hospital and Maternity Center and Our Saviour Rehabilitation Center in 1986, fourteen years before the official inception of the MDGs.

Edeh then founded a home for motherless babies in 1991 and since then, this center has been giving succor to numerous children who may have otherwise died. The reduction of child mortality is the fourth MDG and Fr Edeh's health establishments alleviate not only the sufferings of the poor but also work squarely beyond that. As already emphasized, he started this even before the MDGs were set, as an expression of Edeh's mission of practical and effective charity, to better the lot of others through selfless efforts.

Nwoye (2013) observes that Edeh does not allow abandoned children to be relegated to lives of penury and hunger and this is underscored by Edeh's establishment of Our Saviour Motherless Babies Home. He gathers these children, makes them feel at home, as they would feel in their parents' homes and eventually facilitate the realization of their life dreams because they are *mmadi*. At this point it will be necessary to present many of the health institutions and initiatives founded by Edeh for the healthcare delivery:

Our Saviour Hospital and Maternity, Elele, 1986
Our Saviour Rehabilitation Center, Elele, 1986
Our Saviour Motherless Babies Home, Elele, 1992
Our Saviour Specialist Diagnostic Laboratory, Enugu, 1991
Our Saviour Specialist Diagnostic Laboratory, Okija, 2001
Madonna University Teaching Hospital, Elele Elele, 2002
Caritas University Medical Clinic, Enugu
Madonna University Medical Clinic, Okija
Our Saviour Pharmacy, Elele

Free medication for bishops and advanced priests
Healthcare for the indigent
Rehabilitation Center for the Mentally Retarded
Madonna University Medical Clinic, Akpugo

Edeh makes these selfless contributions to humanity in the pursuit of peace without announcement. Amah (2012) says that he was attracted to researching Edeh's leadership style because of Edeh's humility and preference to hide behind the fame of Jesus rather than to achieve personal media coverage. Amah relates that in his personal interactions with Edeh, the clergyman has emphasized that his primary interest is to inspire and influence people's lives. Edeh therefore sees himself as a mere instrument of God to enable *mmadi* to actualize his good nature and as a mere messenger whose work cannot overshadow the original sender of the message, author and principal actor, Chineke. Praise, according to Edeh, is for God only and not for man.

We can see then that Edeh works for the power of love rather than the love of power. In some countries today, especially third world, malaria, typhoid, and measles are still major killers. The scourge of malaria is a global one. The World Health Organization initiated the Roll Back Malaria (RBM) program in 1998 to stop the agony of this disease. The RBM summit, which was held in Abuja, Nigeria, in the year 2000, sought to enhance the anti-malaria fight in Africa and the choice of Abuja as the venue indicates the problem this epidemic poses not only to Africa but also more specifically to Nigeria which is the most populated country in Africa and the largest black nation in the world.

This summit sought to reduce malaria-related deaths in Africa by at least half by the year 2010 with a combination of preventive and curative measures. These measures in question include the use of insecticides and treated mosquito nets and efforts to keep the environment clean. While WHO's efforts have been commendable, it is still unfortunate that malaria remains a major killer in the third world, especially in Africa.

Since 2000, the year of the Abuja summit, malaria has not yet become a thing of the past. It is still responsible for a relatively high proportion of world deaths annually and Africa remains at high risk, with malaria the most endemic parasitic disease on the continent. With malaria, along with cholera and HIV/AIDS ravaging humanity, especially in Africa, one wonders about the sustainability of health promises and policies made by various local and international institutions.

In "Edehization of the Millennium Development Goals," from *The Actualization of Millennium Development Goals: Fr Edeh as a Pace Setter*, Ezechi Chukwu (2013) observes that malaria, typhoid, and measles continue to hold sway as child killers. Furthermore, child mortality caused by malnutrition and lack of access to drugs is still pronounced. However, Chukwu (2013) emphasizes that Edeh has played a prodigious role in the reduction of child mortality in his endeavour.

Thus, with his multiple healthcare schemes, including hospitals, clinics, departments of medicine and nursing in his universities, scientific laboratories, and courses on environmental studies at his universities, Fr Edeh continues to provide a strong theoretical and practical panacea to the scourge of child mortality. Many children who are treated daily in his hospitals would have probably died had they depended only on public healthcare institutions. In addition, Edeh continues to make wonderful contributions to improved maternal health and combating HIV/AIDs and other diseases, thereby using the machinery of *EPTAism* and ECPM to save lives and bestow peace to the human community. Edeh's philosophy of *mmadi* is manifested in this area, as his continuous struggles to combat HIV/AIDS and to improve on maternal health by and large conform to the African philosophy of being that he developed. For example, a lot of poor expectant mothers receive free treatment in his facilities and HIV/AIDS patients often receive free drugs and these efforts are in agreement with Edeh's mission of practical and effective charity.

The MDGs Report 2012 states that progress on the child mortality front has been made, and according to Sha Zukang, UN under Secretary

General for economic and social affairs, child-survival progress is gaining momentum. There has also been an increase in the treatment of people suffering from HIV/AIDS in the whole regions. The measure to halt tuberculosis is yielding positive results, while deaths as a result of malaria are also being reduced. While the proposed decrease in maternal mortality rates is still far from the 2015 target, there has been improvement in that regard and in maternal health (UN MDGs Report, 2012).

Health is wealth, but an unhealthy person lacks the capacity to realize the fullness of his or her existence. In this regard, the positive results towards MDGs Number 4, 5, and 6 is good news, although the UN should improve on its action plan to achieve more effective global healthcare and governments at all levels should also be mindful to provide health programs to achieve these three MDGs.

In the paper "Science Education and the Achievement of the Millennium Development Goals (MDGs) by 2015," Garba (2009) states: "Very often, efforts to attain the MDG target can inadvertently meet with some challenges. Therefore, there is no simple solution to the problem. It is more productive to understand that a dilemma exists between, on one hand, efforts to achieve the MDGs and on the other hand, efforts to overcome these challenges." Garba further observes that inconsistency in policy formulation and proper coordination of programs could mar institutional administration and policy implementation where it concerns the MDGs.

The fight against HIV/AIDS is a common battle and malaria in particular is a major human killer in sub-Saharan Africa. To concentrate on poverty eradication without giving proper attention to health is to generate counterproductive measures. We must institute vigorous campaigns to prevent these deadly diseases while also putting in place adequate curative measures. The world is an integrated union like the human body, so what affects one part affects the other. Therefore, the whole world must make concerted efforts to achieve good global human health. Mfam explains:

"HIV/AIDS not only affects the individual, it touches entire communities and countries. As more and more teachers die from HIV/AIDS, children are robbed of an education. Farmers dying of HIV/AIDS are unable to provide enough food for their families and villages, causing more poverty and hunger" (2009, 20).

Although there are new drugs that can prolong life for HIV/AIDS patients, there is no drug that can cure this disease so far, therefore were must intensify effort mainly on prevention. People all over the world should be encouraged to embrace formal and sex education; although illiteracy and ignorance do not directly cause diseases, but one cannot deny the fact that illiteracy is a barrier to receiving information about healthcare and behaviours that prevent disease. In this vein, it is imperative that the UN should not be left alone in this battle for world health. Nations, NGOs, civil society organizations, corporations, international organizations, and religious institutions should all contribute to this important quest to enthrone adequate human and environmental healthcare for all.

Evaluations

Irrespective of the general progress made in the health sector, there are still some challenges as evidenced in 2012 UN Report. While Northern Africa for instance has achieved the MDGs target on the Reduction of Child Mortality, on the other hand, sub-Saharan Africa and Oceania, per the report, have achieved only less than half of what is required to reach the set target. In this case, mortality rates for the under-five is still a challenge, just as there is the need to resume progress in the reduction of measles-related mortality as agreed by World Health Assembly in 2010.

It is also noted that the 2015 target on maternal mortality is still far from being realized. Above all, while access to treatment by those who live with HIV has increased, sub-Saharan African on the other hand is left behind (UN MDGs Report, 2012). If these trends are not reversed, the socio-economic progress of the individuals, families, countries, and regions, concerned and by extension, the world in general, will be hampered.

All the eight Millennium Development Goals are intertwined and it is therefore difficult to target the realization of any of them in isolation. For example, maternal health affects child mortality, because the health of a pregnant mother impacts the health of her baby in the womb. Partnership and cooperation are needed to tackle the menace.

It is true that biomedical technologies for screening, scanning and provision of therapy improve maternal health and reduce infant mortality, but such technology does not guarantee the extermination of these problems. Further, the scourge of HIV/AIDS is still very much alive, irrespective of the public sensitization to its effects by media coverage and the efforts of various institutions.

The challenge of the HIV/AIDS pandemic calls for a comprehensive global reappraisal involving individuals, families, religious organizations, healthcare workers, and educators. In this vein, Dabo and Msheliza (2009) call for a guide to avoiding illicit sexual relationships. While families should be deeply involved with the socialization of their children, religious organizations should take up the task of providing their moral grooming. Furthermore, health institutions should partner with the educational sector to organize sensitization workshops and seminars and to hold classes on the causes and effects of HIV/AIDS in schools.

Recommendations from *EPTAism*

Man as *Onye* (Person) Rather than *Ife* (Thing): In his explanation of Igbo metaphysics, Prof. Edeh (1985) makes a systematic inquiry into the Igbo notion of being and describes human being as more closely linked with *onye*, "who," rather than *ife*, "thing/object." For Edeh, Onye in the Igbo grammatical syntax: "unquestionably conveys the idea of a human being" (Ibid: 94).

Edeh lays emphasis on the fact that *onye* can be used as a noun: "In this category, it is nearest but not the exact English equivalent of person" (Edeh 1985, 94); and can also be used to refer to other living entities that are superhuman. The peculiarity of *onye* in this context is that even when it is used as a noun, it normally precedes a noun or an adjective: for example, *Onye nwe?* ("Who is the owner?") and *Onye nwe uwa* ("The owner of the world). Edeh further explains that *onye* conveys the "idea of human being" and that it can be employed to "designate spiritual beings."

In continuation of his analysis, he makes it explicit that the term, 'being' more generally cannot be designated with *onye*:

"In no way can one stretch the Igbo concept of *onye* stretch to embrace things like stones, wood, or iron, etc. If, for instance, a piece of stone fell and broke a plate, an Igbo person would ask, *"Onye kwuwalu afele?"* (who broke the plate?) *Onye* here can never refer to the stone. What it refers to is who, the person who dropped the piece of stone that broke the plate. Hence, Onye is not comprehensive enough to translate the term "being"" (Edeh 1985, 94).

This principal defect of *onye*—that it is unable to denote nonhuman and non spiritual entities—places a dichotomy between the animate and the inanimate. Whereas *onye* has an inbuilt link with the human and animate, *ife*, on the other hand, has a direct link to things. Edeh continues, "The Igbo word *ife* primarily means thing, anything material or immaterial. It is also used to refer to a happening, an event, an occurrence. *Ife* can be affixed to any adjective or a verb to mean a specific thing" (1985, 95). In this regard, it is clear that while a human could be designated with *onye*, he could never be defined as mere *ife* only, for *ife* cannot designate a human being. While we can ask, *Kedu ife bu ihe a?* ("What is this thing?") about objects, we can only say *Onye bu onye a?* ("Who is this person?) for a human. Edeh's healthcare programs put this duality between animate beings and things, subject versus object, principal versus attribute, mainstream versus ephemeral, and, of course, *mmadi* as "good that is" into consideration.

Healthcare in Edeh, whether it works toward MDG Number 4, 5, or 6, considers humans as *mmadi* and as *onye*, not as mere *ife*. This thoughtfulness is key to Edeh's healthcare approach. Edeh concludes that "human beings are the principal focus of the visible world" (1985, 97). Therefore, his healthcare services approach each of those they serve as *onye bu mmmadu* (one who is good that is) and not as *ife nkiti* (a mere thing or object).

Campaign against Premarital Sex: The MDGs Report 2012 states that access to treatment for people living with HIV increased in all regions, to the extent that at the end of 2010, 6.5 million people were receiving antiretroviral therapy for HIV or AIDS in developing regions. However, the report states that the 2010 target of universal access had not been reached. The fundamental question here is that even if the target were reached, is the approach of the MDGs to the prevention of HIV/AIDS viable? Does MDGs seek to condemn premarital sex?

Edeh condemns premarital sex since it degrades the sexual relationship, which is tied to the union between husband and wife. We recall that in Edeh's concept of *omenani*, anything that is at variance with *omenani* is anti-*omenani* as a result, is *aru* (abomination), which usually attracts the expression *tufiakwa* (forbidden). Edeh believes we therefore need to discourage the abuse of sex in this way, especially by youths. These youths will understand the purpose behind this discouragement when they are at the period of biological and social maturity. By doing so, we drastically reduce the potentiality to new infections of HIV/AIDS. Prevention is better than cure, as the saying goes. To reach the MDG target of reduction is one thing, but to discourage it in practical terms and consolidate on the achievement is a different thing altogether.

Discouragement of Sex and Sexism on Campus: Unfortunately, the UN report on MDGs does not take into account the various environments and circumstances in which people and young ones in particular, easily contact HIV/AIDS. With the sense of liberty and maturity that students claim in secondary and tertiary educational institutions, many of them are disposed to engage in sex. They are away from the direct influence of their parents or guardians and this is the age at which they rebel against institutions, authority, and standards. Therefore, they approach sex with recklessness and are exposed to contacting HIV/AIDS and other venereal diseases and this is responsible for the proactive measures adopted in Edeh's institutions.

Discouragement of Illegitimate Sex in General: As a reflection of African philosophy, which is more practical than abstract, Edeh is a crusader against illegitimate sexual relationships. Edeh is opposed to clandestine sexual relations because it could easily lead to many health hazards gross unethical practices. It is obvious that unwanted pregnancy, especially for non-married partners for example is usually vulnerable to abortion, mainly if the baby is rejected by either or both biological parents on account of illegitimacy, inability, or non-preparedness for the baby and this could be morally wrong, thus, can lead to the willful extermination of fetus. How then do we classify this kind of mortality?

There are cases where unmarried ladies and teenagers get pregnant, give birth to the baby, and subsequently abandon the child due to lack of commensurate means of sustaining the baby. This is even equivalent to infanticide and is therefore totally condemnable. Youths are today carriers of venereal diseases and HIV/AIDS more than legitimately married couples because of this laxity towards sex. Is it not better to take a proactive measure as Edeh proffers?

EPTAism, a harmonization of theory and action, condemns all indiscriminate sexual relationships and Edeh outlaws them in all his institutions, both academic and otherwise. Edeh insists that it is better that we avoid those conditions that lead to diseases and other ailments instead of opting to cure them. Students are human beings who are vulnerable in an environment in which they have no direct supervision from their parents or guardians, therefore Edeh guards them so that they and their families and society do not fall victim to the consequences of illicit sex. This is one important area that the UN should reflect on for the realization of MDG Number 6.

Love to Victims of Sickness: Another important area that the UN's MDG Report 2012 did not address is the way that victims of various ailments are catered to and shown love by government authorities. To what extent do governments and other authorities treat them as *mmadi*? Do governments seek to treat them as human beings loved by their Creator, Chineke? Do they ensure that against all odds, the sick are not discriminated against? To what extent are they given a sense of happiness and spiritual renewal? These are the questions Edeh's philosophy answers and his facilities work to implement.

Through his prayer ministry, which is now a National Pilgrimage Center, Edeh gives thousands of people hope and joy irrespective of their state of health. He makes them understand that their tribulations have not in any way taken away their ontological status as "good that is" and loved by their Creator. MDGs in the area of healthcare should therefore be targeted also at showing practical love and kindness to patients.

Responsive Healthcare Initiatives: Edeh prefers prevention to cure, but also provides measures in case the preventable is not prevented. He uses all his medical establishments and healthcare programs to continuously combat child mortality and HIV/HIV/AIDS, malaria, and other diseases. He also uses them every day to improve maternal health. Above all, Fr Edeh uses his health initiatives to revitalize the poor, the downtrodden, and the abandoned living in our midst, often treating them for free.

Edeh: A Paragon of Gender Parity and Women Empowerment

The question of gender equality has taken center stage in the global discourse in the past few decades. Since antiquity, we have lived in a male-dominated world. The Oxford Advanced Learner's Dictionary defines gender as "the fact of being male or female," but there is clearly more to it than that. It poses theoretical concerns and generates a lot of ethical questions as well. For instance, are men and women different and what do they have in common? Do gender issues intersect with other systems of inequality? Is there really a complicated imbalance between the genders in society? Do we still live in a patriarchal society? Are females truly suppressed and discriminated against in every sector of life and every institution? If so, are people working to correct this imbalance?

In short, the issue of gender is surrounded by a myriad of complex questions, but the truth of the matter is that man and woman are ontologically created equal by the Creator. However, the sexes do exhibit different biological features. The individuals who produce sperm cells are generally classified as male while the individuals who produce egg cells are classified as female. Thus, the biologist conceives sex and the sex of a particular individual as being grounded in reproductive processes.

One of the fundamental characteristics of living organisms is their ability to reproduce themselves and this can be done in two ways. The first is the process of asexual reproduction in which part of the organism in effect breaks off from the whole to form a new individual. The amoeba is one organism that reproduces in this manner. In asexual reproduction, the genetic material of the new individual is identical to that of the original organism.

The second type of reproduction, the method that human beings use, is sexual reproduction, in which a new individual is formed from the genetic material contributed by two separate members of the species. This process has the advantage of allowing for greater variability among members of the species and thus a greater chance that they will survive to pass on their genes. For this type of reproduction to happen, the cells that contain the separate sets of genetic material must merge with each other.

When this occurs, the new organism must be nourished until it is sufficiently developed and the egg cell provides this nourishment. The other reproductive cell, called sperm, only penetrates the egg cell and contributes its genetic material. Once this happens, all things being equal, a human male or female is born as an individual whose life is as valid as any other.

In any case, the meaning of male and female in everyday life is quite different from their biological and reproductive sense because, while male and female distinguish each other for the purpose of reproduction, not all people can or wish to reproduce and with the help of new technologies like artificial insemination and embryo transplant, human reproductive methods have changed.

Edeh believes that both male and female share equally the status of *mmadi*, "good that is," given to them by God, who is by nature the absolute good. Edeh states: "I maintain that the Supreme Being, Chineke, is the one who creates and remains present in his creatures, Osebuluwa is the one who cares and supports all beings to realize their purposes. The logical implication here is that God did not only create the world and abandon it but carries it along" (2012, 3–4). To achieve world peace, he recommends African philosophy articulated through Igbo metaphysics, for "this can be achieved when men begin to see man (good that is) as created in the image of God and therefore deserves respect and care" (2012, 4).

These statements from Edeh show that he does not consider the genders to be unequal. He believes that both men and women are products of their Creator, who cares for and provides for them. He is therefore intolerant of discrimination by sex, as it is an offence against both God and humanity. Edeh describes the ideal of human dignity without gender, ethnic, or cultural bias and anchors it in the interplay between thought and action typical of African philosophy.

According to Edeh (2009), the philosophy of ideal human dignity gives people an ideal human existence. The ideal human dignity in question is based upon the believe that all beings created by God are ontologically good, and therefore, deserve respect. Every human being, whether male or female, is given a position of honor, prestige, and inviolable rights because together, they are the principal creatures of the Creator, Chineke.

Edeh is therefore, at the forefront of gender parity and this can be seen in his work even before the MDGs were instituted. In Igbo metaphysics, he developed the God-man-world scheme, which gives a strong foundation to the dignity of human beings and human existence in general. As he states: "African metaphysics is saying that we should accept man as good within the context of creation" (2009, 40).

Today we talk of "natural rights" which are immutable, inviolable and universally applicable, irrespective of gender or other differences. These rights, too, show that men and women share ontological parity. However, this is different from a kind of justifiable social inequality, a situation whereby some people occupy privileged positions in families, organizations and institutions as a result of the rules, regulations, and norms that guide them. Sometimes, some positions, ranks, and cadre are necessary for bureaucratic and administrative purposes but all these should not undermine the ontological equality of all.

Edeh did not say that humans should be considered within the context of gender or any other artificial barrier but put purely as "good that is," *mmadi*, participating in the order of the supreme good in se, that is God. The concept of "good that is" is neither selective nor discriminatory. The good that is knows no race, culture, or location of origin. The "good that is" considers not gender but upholds man and woman as ontological equals in the presence of their maker, Chi-ukwu. To say that man is *mmadi* is to say that woman is *mmadi*. Edeh strongly believes in this reality and works assiduously to treat everyone according to his or her merit rather than his or her gender.

While making a thorough assessment of Fr Edeh's life and leadership style, Amah (2012) describes Edeh as a man who values people, a man who develops people, a man who builds community, a man who displays authenticity and a man who provides leadership and shares leadership. Amah remarks that because Edeh's thinking and actions are in accord with his concept of *mmadi*, he therefore makes the valuing of people an integral part of his vocation, understanding that the goodness in every human person must be sustained. Edeh also continues to develop people since every *mmadi* is naturally invested with potentials deserving of development to full realization.

The ongoing analysis makes it clear that Edeh does not hide his passion for fair play, equality, and justice when it comes to gender-related issues. The number of women he has integrated into the administration of his programs and institutions lends credence to this claim. In his institutions, women have been employed not only on professional merit but also at the highest levels of the bodies they work for. In Edeh's academic institutions, for instance, women hold principal positions such as headmistress, principal, Head of Department, and Dean of Faculties. In the non-academic sector, they have risen to the level of accountants, administrators, and managers.

In Edeh's institutions at large, women have benefitted immensely and continue to benefit. In some cases, the level playing field Edeh has created has made women surpass men in their accomplishments. As Onyewuenyi (2011) points out, the matriculations of Caritas University students between 2007 and 2010 demonstrate that female enrollment in the school is not only on par with that of males but has, surprisingly, surpassed that of males. This is concrete evidence of the empowerment of women at Edeh's institutions and a just way of institutionalizing gender parity without shortchanging these women's male colleagues.

Evaluations

Gender disparities emerge in various ways in the education system, as noted in the MDGs Report 2012 and unless these imbalances are corrected, they may unfortunately become permanent. The report emphasizes that girls face more bottlenecks at the secondary level of education than at the primary level due to discrimination in families and in societies.

The report also states that girls from poor homes are faced with the barriers to education compared with their peers from well-to-do homes. To complicate issues, women still have no access to jobs in some regions, and women are left to resort to informal means of earning a living. Further, even though women continue to gain representation in parliaments, it is still worrisome that the pace is relatively slow, although the situation is generally better there than in appointed positions in the executive arms of government (UN MDGs, 2012). However, it is still necessary that we treat every human being based on merit and not gender.

All socio-cultural inhibitions to the development and emancipation of women need to be dismantled and a socially constructed disabilities and artificial barriers used to discriminate against women need to be jettisoned, for such disabilities are sometimes used to achieve selfish ends. Reisine and Fifield (1988), whose work discusses the concept of disability and health status, state that contrary to the way disability is defined by bodies offering social security, the notion of disability is better understood by the historical definition of the World Health Organization (WHO), which says it is not only the absence of pathology but also social, physical, and psychological functioning.

The WHO goes on to differentiate impairments, disabilities, and handicaps, saying that a disability is a physical phenomenon, whereas a handicap is a culturally defined impairment. While disability refers to a restriction or lack of ability to perform normally, handicap means disadvantage due to impairment or disability.

Recommendations from *EPTAism*

Meritocracy: A Hallmark of Women Empowerment: According to the MDGs Report 2012, women do not have equal access to job opportunities as men in some regions, but Edeh provides men and women with equal opportunities in his employment. As emphasized earlier, Edeh defends hires based on merit, not gender. Amid claims and counterclaims that we live in a male-dominated world, Edeh has taken it as a responsibility to give women the positions they deserve, enabling them to rise to positions at the highest levels of his institutions.

Provision of Education for Women: To ensure that women have the opportunity to develop their potentials, Edeh provides education to girls and women from nursery school to university, establishing Our Saviour Girls Secondary School in Aba in 1990 and OSISATECH Girls Secondary School in Enugu in 1992. This effort is strategically geared towards closing the gap between girl-child and boy-child education and working to accomplish MDGs Number 3.

Automatic Employment on Graduation: As the saying goes, an idle man is the devil's workshop. In the current global economic crisis, it is common sense that education without employment is a recipe for humiliation and social vice. As a way of integrating male and female graduates into the labor market, Edeh often gives them automatic employment in his various outfits. This way, they become assets to the nation early in life. The MDGs should also include policies and programs that could enhance the creation of jobs for graduates to avoid unemployment related social hazards.

Special Weekly Orientation for Students: Greatness starts in the mind and success is determined by the values we appropriate. While some people are motivated from within, others are more inspired from without and Edeh understands the power of inspiration as a key to his own success. For this reason, he has made it mandatory in all his tertiary institutions for students to attend a 3 hour weekly orientation session for such inspiration. At Madonna University in Elele, which has a massive number of students, every Monday morning from 6:00 to 9:00 is specially dedicated to the orientation program for female students (their male counterparts have their session on Tuesdays). Caritas University students in Enugu have the same session on Thursday from 7:00 to 10:00 a.m. One of the merits of this program is that it inspires students to develop self-confidence in order to better their lives and society.

Female students are encouraged to work hard to overcome gender barriers and to see men as their intellectual equals. Through this program, Edeh empowers his students, both male and female, psychologically and intellectually, giving them the necessary mind-set to propel them to success.

The United Nations, through UNESCO, should consider introducing such a program to public schools to enhance the achievement of MDG Number 3.

Edeh: Paragon of Environmental Sustainability

Edeh's environmental sustainability apparatus is built on the following principles:

* The concept of humans as "good that is"
* Sound environmental education in his institutions
* His charitable works across the globe for the survival of humans who are the principal occupants of the environment
* Madonna International Charity Peace Award (MICPA)
* Other operational tools, including *EPTAism*

Nature has necessitated that we rely on our immediate surroundings for food and shelter and our surroundings contain much of what we need. Unfortunately, our environment is being depleted because of our self-centeredness, as we have colonized, dominated, and conquered rather than appreciated and ennobled nature from which we may derive freedom, harmony, and peace.

Regrettably, we no longer act for the common good as we did in the days when communalism was the heartbeat of social cohesion. The human environment is continuously dilapidating due to egoistic policies, unmoderated technological advancement, armed conflict, socioeconomic crisis, and of course natural disaster. Often, our environment suffers because of our self-imposed ecological tragedy.

The Biotic and Abiotic Components of the Environment

The word environment, although we use it every day, is a complex term. Because of our diverse culture, belief, tradition, education, and philosophies of life, we define the word differently and various schools of thought have provided their own simplified definitions. Some define environment as the natural place where people, animals, and plants live. Others define it as the external factors, such as light or the sources of energy influencing the life of organisms. It can also be defined as the conditions surrounding people and affecting the way they live.

However, this word environment, with its stem environ, meaning "surroundings," is perhaps more understandably defined simply as the surroundings in which people live. In these surroundings are everything, both living and nonliving things of all varieties. In strict scientific terms, these living and nonliving things are called biotic and abiotic, respectively. The basic constituents of the environment are water, air, land, plants, and animals, with the non living components, water, air, and land making up the abiotic components and the living components, the animals, plants, and microorganisms, constituting the biotic components.

The natural environment consists of all the living and nonliving things occurring naturally on earth. This environment is essentially self-supporting and requires minimal human management for maintenance without any necessary active or economic inputs from man for its sustenance. It is therefore a complete ecological unity without massive human intervention. The natural environment can be broken down into physical and climatic components. The physical components a those things we can see, touch, and feel, such as hills, mountains, valleys, plains, rivers, lake, seas, coastline, animals, and plants. In contrast, climatic components are things we can sometimes see and feel but can always touch, such as radiation, sunshine, wind, pressure, humidity, precipitation, and clouds.

Organisms constantly interact with their environment and this interaction is necessary for the transfer of energy from one component, biotic or abiotic, to another. Ecosystem is the term generally used to describe this interaction, collaboration, and cooperation of organisms for which by aggregating together, form a community and influence the lives of other organisms.

All those ways humans maltreat the environment have created an ecological calamity. Human activities have led to the destruction of biodiversity, jeopardizing the richness of species and genetic variability. Our environmental impact started long ago, when humans discovered fire and extracted materials from the soil to produce tools for building, cultivating crops, and other activities. In the constant quest to improve their living conditions, humans then devised means of making life more comfortable and convenient by exploiting the natural environment. Later, the Industrial Revolution made a great impact on humanity with the advent of so many different new activities and technologies, automobiles and chemicals in particular, that have taken their toll on the environment.

Today, the world is filled with so many technological products, including aircraft, ships, skyscrapers, luxurious automobiles, and telecommunication devices and sophisticated technologies are now available to industries, including food, textile, chemical manufacturing; agriculture; healthcare; mining, and war, all of which require resources from the environment. However, the environment is vital for our survival and all ecological and evolutionary changes are centered in nature.

Environmental Manipulation by Humans

Our capacity to manipulate our environment has its merits and demerits. The felling of trees is advantageous for construction, but it also leads to drought. With advancements in technology, our environment has become a source of materials for our comfort rather than a wilderness in which we hunted wild animals and sometimes faced threats to our survival. We are now able to communicate with people across states, countries, and continents and machines have made life easier by saving us labor that strains the body. Our industrialization has greatly improved our well-being thanks to environmental manipulation by man.

However, industrialization has led to environmental destruction on a scale never seen in history and humans are systematically wreaking more havoc on the earth and further diminishing its natural resources. In nearly every region, the air is being befouled, the waterways polluted, the soils washed away, the land desiccated, and the wildlife killed. Even the depths of the sea are not immune to pollution. Over time, the carbon and nitrogen cycles upon which all living things, including humans, depend for the maintenance and renewal of life have been irreversibly damaged.

Basically, industry and technology have generated other ecological imbalances as well. We generate radioactive waste, long-living pesticides, and thousands of toxic and potentially toxic chemicals and put them into our food, water, and air. The industries that create them also impact the environment. As cities expand into vast, densely populated urban belts, they further deplete raw materials. At this juncture, we seem to have forgotten that nature is what it is because of a balance between living and nonliving things.

Anything strong and powerful only exerts more and more power if left unchecked and our power over the environment will only expand, leading to more destruction if it is not controlled, worsening the din of noise pollution; the stresses created by congestion; the immense accumulation of garbage, sewage, and industrial waste; and the profligate destruction of precious raw materials. These by-products of industrialization also change natural ecosystem.

For how long shall we continue to compose our requiem? We have done more damage to the planet in a single generation than humans did for thousands of years. Unfortunately, humans continue to destroy nature and destabilize the ecosystem. In this manner, it is out of equilibrium. If the pace of destruction continues, it is terrifying to speculate about what lies ahead for the next generation. This menace may damage the very integrity of life for centuries.

The ecological crisis of the Contemporary Age is worse than man has witnessed at any time in the past and we continue to lose biodiversity. It is therefore critical to emphasize that humanity depends upon the complexity of life and that his well-being and survival depend upon the long evolution of organisms into increasingly complex and interdependent forms.

Nature and *Mmadi*

Homo sapiens is the most developed living species, and our intellect has given us dominance over the earth and we have trampled on all of it. We have refused to understand that the environment is an intrinsic part of our existence, as without the environment, we may not have existed at all or we could have probably remained as spirit only.

Edeh's Metaphysics considers the environment as part of *ife di* (being) and he underlines that all beings are good by virtue of their creation by God, the Supreme Good. Anthropologists Jolly and Plog are on the same page as Edeh, as they state: "Human beings are not separate from nature, or even in nature. Rather, we are of nature, one among its millions of species" (1979, 3).

Mmadi, the human being, depends on nature: "One of the most important manifestations of our position in nature is our dependence on the rest of nature. We, along with every other form of life, are part of a single ecosystem—a cycle of matter and energy that includes all living things and links them to the nonliving" (Jolly and Plog, 1979,

4). In acknowledging the environment's relevance to human nature, Edeh adds to this: "Man is caught up within the boundaries of these two worlds. *Uwa* (the visible world) is evident since it is experienced by senses, especially those of sight and touch. *Ani muo* (the invisible world) is to the Igbo a reality because it is an accepted fact of everyday activity" (1985, 74).

The Existence of Two Worlds in Edeh

The environment should be treated with care and reverence, according to Edeh's philosophy, for as he expounds on the existence of two worlds in Igbo metaphysics, he reminds us that "for the Igbos, that enveloping world is the abode of nonhuman spirits, both good and bad. Some of the good spirits or gods are the earth, sun, sea, sky, and wind go as well as the gods of the chief crops" (1985, 76). Because the Igbos venerate the earth, sun, sea, wind, and sky (the environment), along with the gods of the chief crops the (gods of fertility and nutrition), then there is no question for them about maintaining environmental health. In *Servant-Leader: Emmanuel M.P. Edeh, an Inspiration in Youth Empowerment and Poverty Alleviation*, Onyewuenyi (2011b) relates that Edeh's conceptual framework, like the African of life, is neither atomistic nor analytic but is being holistic and synthetic, concerned with totality, comprehensiveness.

This is because Edeh's philosophy sees reality as an interdependence of the material, humans, environment and the invisible. In other words, reality is rooted in harmonious reciprocity and complementarity between the material and the immaterial. For Edeh puts it this way: "For all beings in the material universe, existence is a dual inter-related phenomenon" (1985, 77).

With this in mind, Africa should develop a policy that "serves the long-term interests of both the environment and economy" (William, 1990, 17). In view of the idea of the harmony between the environment and the unseen, Edeh remarks:

"For the Igbos, there is a functional unity of the physical, utilitarian world with the deified, unchanging world that has shed its materiality. This is the environment in which the Igbo people, like all other African peoples, are born, live, and die. Immersed in this environment, the people naturally develop the conviction of the existence of two worlds. Because they are much more inclined to be practical than speculative, they tend to make the two worlds equally real, as if both were material. Thus, they express the spiritual concepts connected with the invisible world in a material mode" (Edeh 1985, 77).

Odoemene (2009) also reminds us that every person and creature is directly or indirectly in relationship with every other person or thing as beings who share the same ecosystem and therefore we need to maintain the environment and work in harmony. He further notes that what the world needs most today are reconciliation, justice, and peace and as we know, these are the pillars of *EPTAism* and ECPM. In this light, we see that Fr Edeh has devoted his life working on environmental sustainability along with other MDGs.

Because of his African philosophy that pairs words with action, Edeh has made practical contributions to environmental sustainability. In one effort, the Faculty of Environmental Studies at Caritas University in Enugu facilitates ecological enlightenment and crusade against environmental degradation and their students, too, are champions of environmental sustainability.

In this regard, Edeh is servant-leader with the potential to heal himself and others. Onyewuenyi (2011b) comments that a leader such as Edeh is responsible for the development of a healthy environment that enables teaching and studying to promote the practice and learning of civic virtues. Through this avenue, Edeh the servant-leader shows the light on personal, corporate, institutional and public health.

Because of *EPTAism*, the Madonna International Charity Peace Award (MICPA) founded by Fr Edeh has come to be and in an uninterrupted mission of practical and effective charity, the MICPA has traversed the continents of the world on efforts to assist victims of ecological disasters, including the victims of the 2010 earthquake in Haiti, the 2011 tsunami in Cambodia, and the 2012 flood in Calabar, Nigeria. MICPA is usually accompanied with cash prize as a way of encouraging and continuing the works of charity in different circumstances and the beneficiaries have so far received the award (MICPA) worth thousands of dollars.

The MDGs Report 2012 recorded achievement on environmental sustainability but it is observed that a lot still needs to be done. Asia has seen a reduction in forest loss, but the whole world has not reversed the loss. Forests present many advantages, including improvements in the environment as a whole and wildlife. There are economic benefits from tourism and this has led some governments to initiate campaigns for citizens and residents to plant trees.

More of the earth's surface is being protected all the time, even though a biodiversity continues to be lost. The MDG target for drinking water has been realized ahead of schedule, although sub-Saharan Africa is still behind. Moreover, the percentage of urban slum dwellers in developing countries has reduced, although the absolute percentage is still high (UN MDGs Report, 2012).

The environment is essential to human life therefore humans should keep the environment safe for habitation. A healthy environment elongates human life, just as a polluted environment poses a danger to human life. Environmental degradation is sometimes caused by natural disasters, but humans are a principal architect of this menace. It is therefore necessary that every person must be conscious of how his or her actions affect the environment and efforts should be made to keep the environment healthy for human existence, complementing the MDG target with individual and private organizational efforts. The environment is our common home, and deserves to be healthy, for a healthy environment leads to human security.

In essence, human security means safety for people from both violent and non-violent thrusts. It is a condition of being characterized by freedom from pervasive threat to people's rights, their safety or even their lives. It is an alternative way of seeing the world, taking people as its point of reference, rather than focusing exclusively on the security of territory or governments. Like other security concepts—national security, food security (Don Huber, as cited in Ogaba 2004, 76–77).

The sanity of the environment is without question important in this way, since humans are at the center of the environment. Furthermore, human development cannot be realized if humans are not secured because of environmental conditions. Development, as Waterston (1976) defines it, is a multifaceted process that involves changes in structure and attitudes.

It also embraces changes in institutions and the acceleration of economic growth, reduction in inequality and eradication of hunger and poverty. There is an undeniable connection between development, human security, and the environment.

Evaluations

The major challenges to environmental sustainability, according to the MDGs Reports 2012, are the lack of protection for most species, unequal progress between rural areas and urban areas in accessibility to water. In particular, poor sub-Saharan people lack access to clean drinking water more than rich sub-Saharan people, and access to sanitation also varies according to wealth and residence in sub-Sahara Africa too and the target for sanitation is still far from being realized, irrespective of the other improvements in developing regions (UN MDGs Report, 2012). In view of this, it is a global scandal that so many people are still subject to the health hazards associated with lack of sanitation and wealth.

It is unbelievable that in this day and age, people still cannot access clean drinking water. Unfortunately, the incidence of waterborne diseases is still high in Africa. It is common sense that good drinking water is the most fundamental human need, for humans cannot live without clean water. The disparity in sanitation between the rich and the poor is alarming and for the poor to lack access to sanitation is tantamount to a terrible discrimination.

Sustainable development requires that we take a holistic approach to environmental issues, for it is certain that if environmental resources are allowed to be further depleted because of reckless use, humans will suffer both in the short term and in the long term. Our ecosystem must be protected and treated with care if we are to avert man-made and natural disasters.

It is a good a thing, then, that the United Nations has aroused global consciousness about sustainable development. This type of development does not happen by accident as it is usually willed, planned, and sacrificed for. The Brundtland Commission, a world commission on the environment, explains in its 1987 report that sustainable development is development to meet human needs now with consideration for the possibility of future generations to meet their needs as well (WCED, 1987).

To achieve sustainable development, the world must reverse global warming, the increase in world temperature otherwise called climate change, for it causes sea levels to rise and has the potential to increase the intensity of extreme weather events and change patterns of precipitation. The aims of sustainable development may be fantasies if the world does not reverse global warming. Also, "settlement planning is central to ensuring that urban development and management meet sustainable development goals" (UNCHS, 1996, 259).

Perennial Environmental Consciousness: Having seen Edeh's notion of the environment with the environment being a creation of Chineke and therefore good, we know that the environment is part of the philosophy of *mmadi* and deserves care and protection. This philosophy leads to perennial environmental consciousness in *EPTAism*. To achieve MDG 7, the United Nations should start an awareness campaign to deliver this philosophy to all nooks and crannies of the world, just as Edeh does through his religious ministry, academic institutions, and other outlets.

Provision of Sanitary Facilities: As we noted earlier, one of the earlier challenges noted in the MDGs Report 2012 is the continual lack of access to sanitation, which poses many health hazards to people around the globe. It is unfortunate that people must still defecate outdoors. The United Nations should collaborate with the governments of the world to formulate policies making it mandatory for organizations and institutions of service to the public to provide toilets for the staff members and visitors. Edeh's institutions all have such facilities.

Accessibility to Clean Drinking Water: According to the MDGs Report 2012, some people in sub-Saharan Africa still lack access to clean drinking water irrespective of the fact that water is necessary for human life. In order to overcome this, Edeh's ministry produces Pilgrim Water, which is certified as good for drinking and available in all his institutions.

Provision of Staff Accommodations: No individual can afford to provide accommodation to the whole world, though shelter is a basic human need. Edeh provides accommodation to a good number of his employees and their families for their comfort and security. The United Nations should encourage other institutions to offer similar accommodations in order to facilitate MDGs Number 7.

Environmental Studies: Since the environment is fundamental to human existence, Edeh has made the study of the environment an integral academic program at his tertiary institutions. These programs inform the public about environmental issues, thus contributing to the checking of environmental hazards. Caritas University in Enugu has a faculty of environmental studies which also serves as a crusader of environmental cleanliness. In this vein, the UN should encourage the adoption of environmental education in universities for easier actualization of MDGs Number 7.

Edeh: Champion of Global Partnerships for Development

The collaboration of world countries, especially developed countries with developing countries, is a key MDG. With the level of economic disparity between developed and developing countries, it is certain that more than mere political rhetoric is required to achieve this goal.

Humans have devised means of understanding, dominating, and conquering nature and the universe. We have explored almost every part of our planet and have turned our focus to outer space. The world has witnessed continuous progress in science and technology to solve human problems and improve living condition of people around the world. The present day is distinct from previous era because of our focus on science and technology and today, science and technology provide hope for the future of humanity. Despite this hope, however, science and technology also provide us with anxiety. Wars around the world in the modern Age have been fought with weapons made fierce by science and technology and some countries today are engaged in a constant show of strength through nuclear armaments and other weapons of mass destruction.

Countries of the world have seen many benefits from the good scientific and technological achievements. Mechanization in agriculture has come to stay and factories can mass produce goods and services. Because of science and technology, the world has witnessed a revolution in mass media and telecommunications. The question that still puzzles a rational mind, then, is why the world is still divided between rich and poor despite these advancements. Why are some people still dying of hunger while others have plenty? In short, can the MDGs actually succeed in the development of international partnerships which could reasonably close the gap between the rich and poor nations? Only time will tell.

Edeh's Philosophy of *Mmadi*:
The Key to International Partnerships

Edeh has strategically built mechanisms for global partnership development. He has established a chain of international partnerships for human development in line with his idiosyncrasies. While countries of the world often wait to develop partnerships because of bureaucratic inefficiency, financial assistance from international financial institutions and other forms of aid from richer countries, Edeh's personal measures do not suffer from such delays. Everyone knows how difficult it is to service international debts, not to mention to fully repay them. Must people stand with their arms folded as they wait for international cooperation in this manner?

For the advancement of international growth and relationships, which are the fundamental aims of MDGs Number 8: Development of Global Partnership for Development, Edeh strategically embarks on practical, humanitarian, religious, and empowerment initiatives. At the center of exercise is his philosophy of *mmadi*, which puts into consideration the oneness of man in the world irrespective of his geographical location.

Edeh's human capital development initiatives, transnational charity, religious foundation, academic institutions, multidimensional empowerment schemes, and Justice, Reconciliation, and Peace Center could not have come to be if he had not conceived of humans as *mmadi*. Through his Mission of Practical and Effective Charity in symmetry with *EPTAism*, these efforts have led to extensive human development in different parts of the world, thereby strengthening international partnerships.

MICPA: A Medium for International
Development and World Peace

The Madonna International Charity Peace Award (MICPA) recognizes those who not only do charitable works but also promote charity in any part of the world, and, as Ezechi Chukwu (2013) remarks, it is geared towards global partnerships for development.

Through MICPA, Fr Edeh provides financial support across nations and continents as he honors those distinguished agents of charity. The MICPA, which is an annual event usually held annually in November at Madonna University, Elele. MICPA contributes in no small way to international development, as it has benefitted victims of earthquakes, motherless babies homes, victims of tsunamis, victims of floods, and many more people.

Edeh's Approach to Employment: Aimed at International Cooperation, Development and World Peace

Edeh the thinker and philosopher contributes strategically to the building of global partnerships for development through his approach to employment, which cuts across countries and continents. Edeh, through African philosophy, is committed to giving gainful employment to people across the globe and these efforts institutionalize oneness in the global family and enhance practical developmental partnerships among nations. On his payroll are nationals of Nigeria, Cameroon, the Philippines, Germans and more nationals reflecting Fr Edeh's peculiar commitment to international cooperation and world peace.

With the coming together of all these employees from different parts of the globe, Edeh has succeeded in making his institutions in general a community of *mmadi* in which cultures converge, interact and develop together with the aim of achieving peace. This is possible because the heartbeat of these relationships is love and care for others.

Hossein Daneschumand, a physician from Germany who specializes in obstetrics and gynecology, has been on the medical team at Madonna University Teaching Hospital for some years. He says of his employment: "I came to Madonna University Teaching Hospital through the instrumentality of Rev Fr Prof Edeh. He visited my hospital in Germany and in the course of our interaction I discovered there was agreement of interest, what I mean here is the interest to care for others" (The Saviourites Magazine 2012/2013, 28). Daneschumand's testimony shows Edeh's desire to care for others and to build bridges across nations.

Education in Edeh: Key to Global Partnership Development

Edeh insists that his students carry the values of peace and love into the world with them after graduation, so Edeh the teacher imparts *EPTAism* to his students. Thousands of those students of his tertiary educational institutions are now gainfully employed around the world, preaching and practicing the precepts of *EPTAism* learned from Fr Founder.

National Pilgrimage Center/National Shrine: A Religious Dimension to Global Partnership for Development

Another important dimension to Global Partnership for Development within the Edehist context is the Pilgrimage Center of Eucharistic Adoration and Special Marian Devotion in Elele, which was elevated to the status of a National Pilgrimage Center, a national shrine, on 30 November 2012, making it the first of its kind in Africa. The ceremony was presided over by the Papal Nuncio in Nigeria, His Excellency the Most Rev Augustine Kasujja, who led the celebration of the solemn Eucharist.

This pilgrimage center attracts the faithful from all over Africa and many other parts of the world, who go there to pray and return to give testimonies of how their prayers have been answered. When one asks God for prosperity God and God answers that prayer, the success extends to the society in which that person lives. So, all those pilgrims from around the world return home empowered, revived, and rebuilt. Thus, they are better, able to improve their lives and contribute to the development of their countries and to society in general.

Furthermore, what a thing stands for determines why it is sought after. Edeh stands for care, love, and peace and the ideals of charity, reconciliation, justice, and peace which are preached at the pilgrimage center. Certainly, these are the virtues which the people who flock there pray to achieve.

Thus, adding to Edeh's practical contributions to the development of global partnership. Humans are spiritual and moral beings and to undermine this essential nature is to misconstrue them for objects. By adding a religious dimension to global partnership for development, Edeh integrates important ingredient to his pro MDGs related agenda.

The realization of MDG Number 8: Development of Global Partnership for Development is fundamental to the realization of all the other MDGs, for they all require the collaboration of UN member nations, especially the help of the developed nations. The MDGs Report 2012 notes increased access to the international market for developing countries because of a reduction in barriers to those markets by developed countries. The report also notes that the least developed countries now benefit from preferential treatment from richer countries. Also, developing countries now boast of a rise in cell phone subscriptions and a downward trend in developing countries' debts (UN MDGs Report, 2012).

The world today is a global community a thanks to modern technology, especially in communication and transportation, countries' borders are more open and countries of the world become more interdependent and work in collaboration, having realized that no nation can survive in isolation no matter how rich it is. Richer countries should understand that they need the developing countries' economies as avenues for investment and new markets for their products. Placing stringent barriers on developing countries will not benefit developed nations much. Therefore, it is commendable that such constraints have been reduced, according to the MDGs Report 2012.

In the paper "Renewing the Commonwealth for the 21st Century: Policy Perspectives," Oduntan and Akinrinade (2004) ascribe to international organizations the need to work towards the development of their member nations, as the need for development is the major problem confronting many nations and Africa in particular, hence the establishment of the New Partnership for Africa's Development (NEPAD).

To accomplish MDGs Number 8, other existing international agencies such as FAO, UNESCO, UNICEF, IMF, WTO, WHO, IBRD, ILO, and WFP should give consistent support to nations and cooperate with one another to fast-track the achievement of the other MDGs and they should ensure that their programs are not opposed to the aims and achievements of the MDGs.

For the sake of clarity, Article 1(3) of the United Nations Charter (1945) states that the purpose of the UN, among other things, is the achievement of international cooperation in solving international problems of an economic, social, cultural, and humanitarian nature. Furthermore, the UN seeks to promote respect for human rights and to seek fundamental freedoms for all peoples of the world without distinction by sex, race, language, or religion. The world today is under the canopy of the UN and because of that, all its agencies should complement one another to promote peace and security throughout the world.

Evaluations

Decline in average tariffs have been recorded only for agricultural products in 2010, in the realm of exports from developing countries and the least developed countries, according to the MDGs Report 2012. While a good percentage of Internet users are now in developing countries, rates of use are behind in Africa, especially in sub-Saharan Africa. The decline of debt burdens in some regions is evident, although a decline in export earnings continues. International monetary policy should be restructured to integrate the developing countries into the global market in a more meaningful way.

The fact that average tariffs have declined for agricultural products only poses a great challenge. The problem of debt is also a major constraint to development and the conditions attached to such debts sometimes render the debt counterproductive. Sub-Saharan Africa is continuously behind according to many accepted international indices. It is therefore important that international policies be formulated to carry sub-Saharan Africa along in ongoing global development efforts.

With honest commitment, collaboration and dedication, the MDGs could bring about a worthwhile paradigm shift to the world, but efforts to accomplish the entire package go beyond words. To accomplish MDGs Number 8, which is the creation of a partnership for international development, developed countries must make some sacrifices and participate with goodwill, as "simply providing aid and debt relief without changing the rules of the game is not a solution to global poverty. Justice and sustainability are better long-term solutions than benevolence" (Ugorji, 2009, 71).

Industrialized nations should also reshape international trade in order to meaningfully accommodate the developing nations and they must act in genuine solidarity, recognizing that the best way to provide aid is to guide the latter towards self reliance rather than perpetual dependence.

This is certain because to be the principal agent of one's own development is a route to sustainable growth. The developing countries therefore, need to be empowered in the process of achieving the partnership for global development, for if they are perennial receivers only, the partnership will be lopsided.

Recommendations from *EPTAism*
Humanity as the Focus of Development

Edeh's philosophy places humans squarely at the center of development. The global developmental divide between north and south exists partly because the world is yet to adopt the Edehist notion of human as "good that is" and these unnecessary barriers that humans have created for selfish political reasons only further fan the embers of developmental imbalance and economic disparity between countries of the world. The world must accept that "good that is" is the same all over the globe.

It is quite difficult for the world to achieve a full-fledged global partnership for development unless humanity's ontological status is acknowledged. Edeh is of the conviction that the moment humans are genuinely accepted as *mmadi* by the international community, all efforts toward the achievement of international partnership and development will be successful. This is what Edeh believes in, stands for and has practiced for close to three decades, achieving practical results.

Creation of Jobs: Better than Aid and Loans from International Financial Institutions

While some thinkers, politicians, consultants, and economists think that aid from international financial institutions to developing countries is the ultimate solution, Edeh believes instead that the creation of jobs for all categories of workers is a sustainable antidote to underdevelopment and economic gaps between nations, for debts usually weigh down the pace of development in the indebted countries.

The situation is worse if the borrowing government is corrupt, which is common. Such countries consequently suffer and servicing or repaying the loan becomes impossible. This is why Edeh, in the application of his philosophy that harmonizes thought and action, prefers to create jobs. Edeh has carried out this task for almost three decades and the results are amazing. The UN should consider re-strategizing its policies for accomplishing the MDGs, by embracing job creation for development as an alternative to governments procuring loans from the likes of Paris Club because of the devastating consequences of such loans, especially when they could not be serviced or paid.

Review of Internet Liberalization

The UN has recorded overwhelming achievements in telecommunications n general and in global access to the Internet in particular. However, these achievements should be furthered with care. The world should not be distracted by the proliferation of modern communication to the extent that it ignores technology's inherent drawbacks. A situation in which youths have uncontrolled access to obscene materials on the Internet is alarming. This is not the type of advancement an international partnership for development should aim at.

Therefore, efforts should be made to control access to materials on the Internet with a focus on morality, for we should also talk of spiritual and moral developments, not just material developments alone. This is another component of *EPTAism* that the UN should consider for the sake of a better world and genuine development across the board.

The Peculiarity of the MICPA

The MICPA is a powerful tool that Edeh uses to complete his mission of practical and effective charity internationally. The MICPA is a special effort because of the special recognition it provide along with practical support for those who are at the forefront of charity anywhere in the world. To accomplish the MDGs, the UN should try to design a similar framework like the MICPA, so as to assist those who are genuinely involved with charity.

Funding fake NGOs and other bastardized political organizations NGOs operating under the guise of humanitarian groups does not achieve development. The activities of these groups need to be periodically assessed in order to ascertain the legitimacy and efficacy of their work, before they could receive funding from UN-related donor agencies. Through the MICPA, Edeh targets those who are involved with genuine practical activities to this end.

Through the MICPA, Edeh humbly adds value to a global partnership for development and shows that such a partnership does not have to be concerned only with the signing of agreements. Development is meaningful only when it achieves human growth by considering the ontological nature of humans irrespective of location. This is what Edeh champions through awarding the MICPA without considering religion, ethnicity, country, academic qualification, profession, or skin color. The advancement of the welfare of *mmadi* anywhere through genuine charity is the focus of the MICPA.

Religion as an Agent of International Development

Finally, Edeh adds to the international partnership for development from a religious dimension because he regards humans as spiritual beings, and their development must also be considered from a spiritual dimension. Through the National Pilgrimage Center, he enhances the spiritual and moral lives of people from around the world. Hence, reverend fathers, reverend sisters, reverend brothers, nuns, monks, and other religious leaders work in his religious foundations throughout the world to spiritually form people and perpetuate *EPTAism* and Edeh's mission of practical and effective charity.

Conclusion

In the final analysis, it is obvious that Edeh has contributed his quota in the pursuit of global development. He has demonstrated that it is possible to attain a credible level of healthcare especially amongst the poor and the weak; he has equally set the pace for actualization of the much desired world peace through his various empowerment and charity schemes.

As the adage goes "experience is the best teacher," the various global stakeholders in this mission of actualizing the MDGs should corroborate Edeh's working principles into the global plan since he had started this mission fifteen years before its official declaration.

General Conclusion

The walk to civilization, the walk to greatness, the walk to progress and peace, the walk of humanity has not been rosy. It has not been an easy walk. Man, the "centre" of the universe is a being saddled with responsibility. His nature, reason says that and the holy books corroborate it. Thus, nobody, no age is to be exempted or excused from the mess and misery, rancor, and disunity bedeviling the human community and most importantly in our age.

The United Nations since its inception has indeed done a lot. Veracity and noble are the minds that established it and its principles. However, in the management of human life and cooperation in the global family, UN is usually handicapped in implementation of its policies and programs due to bureaucracy, ego battle and selfishness on the part of major players. As a result, most of its lofty ideals and programs are but mere polemics—serving but the ego and domineering tendencies of the few over the many.

As have seen, there is a disparity, a lacuna between the dream, the thought and the real operations of the UN's Millennium Development Goals. The map is not the road. An accurate map with no good, or wrong road is ineffective, may not take you to the target destination. Likewise a good road, or right road with wrong map is but misleading. There must be a balance between thought and action for there to be effectiveness. And we have also noted that not all that is effective is life giving, peace generating and sustaining. Thus, as it is important that UN's Millennium Development Goals programs should continue, it will be an expression of our humanity to borrow and integrate what one of us, Edeh is offering us to rejuvenate, to imbue or innovate the MDGs with new and life-giving ideas and principles as espoused in philosophy of *mmadi* and *EPTAism* for rapid realization of the desired goals.

From the presentation and assessment of Edeh's contributory strides to the development of humanity fifteen years before the birth of Millennium Development Goals, it is right and good to reason and accept that his philosophy of *mmadi*, which has as its operational principle as Edeh's Philosophy of Thought and Action (*EPTAism*) is a classic and timely in its arrival. The acknowledgement of man as *mmadi* "good that is" is and should be the beginning of whatever program and policies for and with man for his development and peace. Most remarkably is the fact that *mmadi* philosophy naturally coheres with purposeful life-giving actions. It has a necessary connection. This explains why with no world summit and before coming to be of MDGs, Edeh has not only single handedly thought out MDGs but has for more than three decades now actualized to an enviable height every item in the UN's Millennium Development Goals.

REFERENCES

Agbo, Edmund Ugwu. 2012. In *Edeh's Charity Peace Model (ECPM)* First and Second Edition, Edited by Nicholas N. Chukwuemeka. Enugu. Madonna University Press.

Amah, Peter. O. 2012. *Inspiring 21st Century Africans to Serve First*. Enugu: Madonna University Press.

Chibueze, O. G. 2009. "Improvisation and Utilization of Infrastructural" Materials in Primary English Pedagogy: A Key to Achieving the Millennium Development Goals in Nigeria by 2015.

The Voice of Teachers, Teachers without Borders, Africa Regional Chapter, Abuja.

Chukwu, Ezechi, ed. 2012. *Aspects of Edeh's Philosophy. Vol. 2*. Madonna University Press, Enugu.

Dabo, Lydia and Msheliza, Esther. 2009. "The Realization of the Millennium Development Goals (MDGs): The Association of Teachers Against HIV/AIDS Model." The Voice of Teachers, Teachers without Borders, Africa Regional Chapter, Abuja 1 (1).

Edeh, E. M. P. 1985. *Towards an Igbo Metaphysics.* Chicago. Loyola University Press.

———. 2006. *Peace to the Modern World: A Way Forward Through the Concrete Living of the Existential Dictates of the African Philosophy of Being.* Banbury, UK. Minuteman Press.

———. 2009. *Igbo Metaphysics: The First Articulation of African Philosophytion of Being.* Enugu. Madonna University Publications. blicati

———. 2012 Edeh's Charity Peace Model. Enugu. Madonna University Press. Enugu.

Egbekpalu, Purissima. 2011. "The Philosophical Anthropology of Edeh: An Existential Pathway to Global Peace, (In Aspects of Edeh's Philosophy vol. 2, edited by Ezechi Chukwu), Enugu. Madonna University Press.

Garba, C. M. 2009. "Science Education and the Achievement of the Millennium Development Goals (MDGs) by 2015." The Voice of Teachers, Teachers without Borders, Africa Regional Chapter, Abuja.

Glanville, ed., *The Gospel and Globalization: Exploring the Religious Roots of a Globalized World* (Vancouver, B.C., Canada: Regent College Publishing, Joseph Gremillion, Food/Energy and the Major Faiths (Maryknoll, New York. Orbis Books, 1978.

James D. Wolfensohn, "Forward," Gerrie ter Haar, ed., Religion and Development, xvii.

Jolly, C. J., and Plog, F. 1979. *Physical Anthropology and Archeology.* New York: Alfred A. Knopf.

———. 2005. *An Introduction to Philosophy.* London: Continuum. Mfam, K. I. 2009. "Vocational and Technical Education: A Panacea for Achieving the Millennium Development Goals in Nigeria." The Voice of Teachers, Teachers without Borders, Africa Regional Chapter, Abuja.

Nze, C. B., ed. 2011. *Aspects of Edeh's Philosophy.* Vol. 1, Enugu: Madonna University Press.

Odoemene, A. N. 2009, "The Millennium Development Goals and the Church Service to Reconciliation, Justice and Peace in Africa;" In *The Church of Jesus the Saviour in Africa, Vol. 1* (Lineamenta), organized and edited by E. M. P. Edeh. Enugu: Madonna University Press.

Oduntan, Tunde and Akinrinade, Sola. 2004. "Renewing the Commonwealth for the 21st Century: Policy Perspectives"; Nigerian Journal of International Affairs.

Printed in the United States
By Bookmasters